AI FOR TV INDUSTRY

Rakesh Kumar

To all the wives in this world,

This book is dedicated to you, the unsung heroes who tirelessly hold the fort, nurture families, and create homes filled with love, warmth, and laughter. You are the champions of every house, the pillars of strength, and the heartbeats of our lives.

Amidst the hustle and bustle of daily life, you seamlessly juggle countless responsibilities, effortlessly balancing work, family, and personal aspirations. Your unwavering support, selfless sacrifices, and boundless love are the foundation upon which our homes are built.

In every household, you play a myriad of roles - from caregiver and homemaker to mentor and confidante. You are the silent force that keeps our lives running smoothly, the beacon of hope in times of darkness, and the source of endless inspiration.

As we embark on this journey exploring the transformative potential of artificial intelligence (AI) in the TV industry, we recognize and celebrate your invaluable contributions. This book is a tribute to your strength, resilience, and unwavering dedication to the well-being of your loved ones.

In the world of television, AI is reshaping the way we consume content, interact with technology, and connect with the world around us. Through the lens of AI, we uncover new possibilities, redefine entertainment experiences, and create innovative solutions to enhance our lives.

As we delve into the realm of AI for the TV industry, we honor your role as the heartbeat of our homes and acknowledge the countless ways in which you enrich our lives with your love, wisdom, and grace.

Thank you for being the cornerstone of our families, the driving force behind our success, and the epitome of strength and resilience. This book is dedicated to you, with love and gratitude, for all that you are and all that you do.

CONTENTS

INTRODUCTION

Welcome to the forefront of innovation in the television industry, where artificial intelligence (AI) is revolutionizing the landscape of television manufacturing, content delivery, and user experience. In this book, we delve into the transformative potential of AI applications tailored specifically for the TV industry, exploring how cutting-edge technologies are reshaping every aspect of television, from production to consumption.

The advent of Smart TVs and the proliferation of streaming platforms have ushered in a new era of connectivity and interactivity, blurring the lines between traditional television and digital media. With AI at the helm, TVs are evolving beyond mere display devices, becoming intelligent hubs that understand, adapt, and personalize content delivery to meet the diverse needs and preferences of users.

In this comprehensive guide, we embark on a journey through the myriad ways in which AI is reshaping the TV industry. From optimizing manufacturing processes and supply chain management to enhancing content discovery and user interface design, AI-driven solutions are driving innovation and efficiency at every turn.

Through real-world case studies, practical examples, and hands-on tutorials, we uncover the underlying principles of AI technologies and their application in the TV industry. Whether you're a TV manufacturer, content creator, broadcaster, or consumer, this book serves as a roadmap for navigating the AI-driven future of television, equipping you with the knowledge and tools needed to thrive in an ever-evolving landscape.

Join us as we explore the limitless possibilities of AI for the TV industry and unlock the full potential of television as a medium for entertainment, information, and communication in the digital age.

THE ROLE OF AI IN MODERN MANUFACTURING

The role of Artificial Intelligence (AI) in modern manufacturing is transformative, revolutionizing traditional methods and processes across the industry. AI is not merely a technological advancement; it's a catalyst for innovation, efficiency, and competitiveness. Here's a detailed exploration of the various facets of AI's role in modern manufacturing:

1. Process Optimization: AI algorithms analyze vast amounts of data generated throughout the manufacturing process to identify patterns, inefficiencies, and opportunities for improvement. By optimizing production workflows, AI minimizes waste, reduces downtime, and enhances overall productivity.

2. Predictive Maintenance: One of the significant applications of AI in manufacturing is predictive maintenance. By continuously monitoring equipment conditions and performance indicators in real-time, AI systems can predict potential failures before they occur. This proactive approach minimizes unplanned downtime, reduces maintenance costs, and extends the lifespan of machinery.

3. Quality Control and Assurance: AI-powered computer vision systems can detect defects and anomalies in products with remarkable accuracy. By automating quality control processes,

manufacturers can ensure that only products meeting the highest standards are shipped to customers, thus reducing waste and improving customer satisfaction.

4. Supply Chain Management: AI enables manufacturers to optimize their supply chains by predicting demand, identifying potential bottlenecks, and optimizing inventory levels. By leveraging AI-driven forecasting models, manufacturers can minimize stockouts, reduce carrying costs, and enhance overall supply chain efficiency.

5. Customization and Personalization: With AI, manufacturers can efficiently customize products to meet the specific needs and preferences of individual customers. By analyzing customer data and market trends, AI systems can recommend personalized product configurations and design modifications, enabling manufacturers to offer highly tailored solutions to their customers.

6. Human-Robot Collaboration: AI-powered robots and cobots (collaborative robots) are increasingly being used in manufacturing environments to perform a wide range of tasks, from repetitive assembly to complex machining operations. By augmenting human workers with AI-driven automation, manufacturers can improve efficiency, safety, and flexibility on the factory floor.

7. Energy Efficiency and Sustainability: AI algorithms can optimize energy consumption by identifying opportunities for energy savings and minimizing waste in manufacturing processes. By optimizing equipment usage, scheduling, and resource allocation, AI contributes to reducing the environmental footprint of manufacturing operations.

8. Quality Management and Compliance: AI systems can analyze vast amounts of data to ensure compliance with regulatory standards and industry-specific requirements. By automating compliance checks and audits, manufacturers can mitigate risks

associated with non-compliance and maintain high levels of quality and safety.

9. Continuous Improvement and Innovation: AI enables manufacturers to embrace a culture of continuous improvement and innovation by providing valuable insights and actionable intelligence derived from data analysis. By leveraging AI-driven analytics, manufacturers can identify emerging trends, anticipate market shifts, and stay ahead of the competition.

In summary, the role of AI in modern manufacturing is multifaceted, encompassing process optimization, predictive maintenance, quality control, supply chain management, customization, human-robot collaboration, energy efficiency, sustainability, compliance, and innovation. By harnessing the power of AI, manufacturers can unlock new levels of efficiency, agility, and competitiveness in today's rapidly evolving manufacturing landscape.

TV MANUFACTURING INDUSTRY

The television (TV) manufacturing industry is a significant sector within the broader consumer electronics manufacturing landscape. It involves the production of televisions, which are electronic devices used for entertainment, information, and communication purposes. Here's an overview of the TV manufacturing industry:

1. Market Overview: The TV manufacturing industry is a crucial component of the global consumer electronics market. It encompasses a wide range of companies, from multinational corporations to smaller, specialized manufacturers. The industry is characterized by intense competition, rapid technological advancements, and shifting consumer preferences.

2. Key Players: Major players in the TV manufacturing industry include multinational corporations such as Samsung, LG Electronics, Sony, Panasonic, and TCL. These companies have a significant market presence and invest heavily in research and development to innovate and stay competitive.

3. Product Range: TVs manufactured by industry players come in various types, sizes, and technologies. This includes traditional LED/LCD TVs, OLED TVs, QLED TVs, and increasingly popular smart TVs. Manufacturers continually introduce new features and functionalities to attract consumers, such as high-resolution displays, advanced audio systems, smart home

integration, and internet connectivity.

4. Manufacturing Process: The manufacturing process for TVs is complex and involves multiple stages. It typically includes component sourcing, assembly, testing, quality control, packaging, and distribution. Key components such as display panels, processors, circuit boards, and casings are sourced from suppliers and assembled into finished products in manufacturing facilities.

5. Technology Trends: The TV manufacturing industry is heavily influenced by technological trends and innovations. Advancements in display technologies, such as OLED (Organic Light-Emitting Diode) and QLED (Quantum Dot Light Emitting Diode), have led to improvements in picture quality, color accuracy, and energy efficiency. Additionally, the integration of smart features, including internet connectivity, streaming services, voice control, and artificial intelligence, is becoming increasingly common in modern TVs.

6. Global Market Dynamics: The TV manufacturing industry is subject to various global market dynamics, including economic conditions, consumer spending trends, trade policies, and technological advancements. Emerging markets, such as China and India, represent significant growth opportunities due to rising disposable incomes and increasing demand for consumer electronics.

7. Challenges and Opportunities: The TV manufacturing industry faces several challenges, including intense competition, pricing pressures, supply chain disruptions, and technological obsolescence. However, there are also opportunities for growth and innovation, particularly in emerging markets, niche segments (such as ultra-high-definition and curved TVs), and new technologies (such as 8K resolution and flexible displays).

8. Sustainability and Environmental Concerns: As with any

manufacturing industry, sustainability and environmental concerns are increasingly important considerations for TV manufacturers. Efforts to reduce energy consumption, minimize waste, recycle materials, and adhere to environmental regulations are becoming integral parts of the manufacturing process.

In conclusion, the TV manufacturing industry is a dynamic and competitive sector within the consumer electronics market. It is driven by technological advancements, changing consumer preferences, and global market dynamics. Despite facing challenges, such as intense competition and technological disruption, the industry continues to innovate and evolve to meet the demands of consumers worldwide.

IMPORTANCE OF AI FOR EFFICIENCY AND QUALITY IMPROVEMENT

The importance of Artificial Intelligence (AI) for efficiency and quality improvement in various industries, including manufacturing, cannot be overstated. Here are some key reasons why AI plays a crucial role in enhancing efficiency and ensuring high quality:

1. Data Analysis and Insights: AI enables the analysis of large volumes of data generated throughout the manufacturing process. By processing this data, AI systems can identify patterns, trends, and correlations that human analysts may overlook. These insights help manufacturers optimize processes, minimize waste, and enhance overall efficiency.

2. Predictive Maintenance: AI-driven predictive maintenance systems use machine learning algorithms to monitor equipment conditions and predict potential failures before they occur. By analyzing data from sensors and historical maintenance records, AI systems can identify early warning signs of equipment degradation and schedule maintenance activities proactively. This minimizes unplanned downtime, reduces maintenance costs, and prolongs the lifespan of machinery.

3. Quality Control and Assurance: AI-powered computer vision systems can inspect products with remarkable accuracy, detecting defects and anomalies that may not be visible to the human eye. By automating quality control processes, manufacturers can ensure that only products meeting the highest standards are shipped to customers. This reduces the risk of product recalls, improves customer satisfaction, and enhances brand reputation.

4. Process Optimization: AI algorithms can optimize manufacturing processes by analyzing data from various sources, such as production equipment, sensors, and supply chain systems. By identifying inefficiencies and bottlenecks, AI systems can recommend adjustments to production workflows, scheduling, and resource allocation. This improves productivity, reduces cycle times, and lowers production costs.

5. Supply Chain Management: AI enables manufacturers to optimize their supply chains by predicting demand, identifying potential disruptions, and optimizing inventory levels. By analyzing data from sales forecasts, supplier performance metrics, and logistics networks, AI systems can recommend optimal inventory levels, transportation routes, and sourcing strategies. This improves supply chain efficiency, reduces stockouts, and minimizes carrying costs.

6. Customization and Personalization: AI-driven recommendation systems can analyze customer data and preferences to recommend personalized product configurations and design modifications. This enables manufacturers to offer highly tailored solutions to individual customers, enhancing customer satisfaction and loyalty.

7. Energy Efficiency and Sustainability: AI algorithms can optimize energy consumption by analyzing data from production equipment and building systems. By identifying opportunities for energy savings and minimizing waste, AI

systems can reduce carbon emissions, lower utility costs, and promote sustainable manufacturing practices.

In summary, AI plays a critical role in improving efficiency and ensuring high quality in manufacturing by enabling data-driven decision-making, predictive maintenance, automated quality control, process optimization, supply chain management, customization, and sustainability initiatives. By harnessing the power of AI, manufacturers can gain a competitive edge, reduce costs, and enhance customer satisfaction in today's rapidly evolving business environment.

BASIC PRINCIPLES OF TV MANUFACTURING PROCESSES

The manufacturing process of televisions (TVs) involves several stages, each crucial for producing high-quality, functional devices. Here are the basic principles of TV manufacturing processes:

1. Component Sourcing: TV manufacturing begins with the procurement of various components required for assembling the television set. These components include display panels (such as LCD, LED, OLED, or QLED panels), circuit boards, processors, memory modules, power supplies, speakers, casings, and other electronic parts. Manufacturers may source these components from multiple suppliers, both domestic and international, based on factors like quality, cost, and availability.

2. Assembly: Once the components are sourced, the assembly process begins. This typically involves the integration of various electronic parts onto a chassis or frame to form the basic structure of the television set. Skilled workers or automated assembly lines perform tasks such as soldering, wiring, and mounting components onto the chassis according to precise specifications and design requirements.

3. Display Panel Integration: The display panel is a critical component of a TV, determining its visual quality and performance. Depending on the type of panel (LCD, LED, OLED,

etc.), specialized processes are involved in integrating the panel into the TV assembly. This may include bonding the panel to the chassis, connecting it to the control circuitry, and ensuring proper alignment for optimal viewing angles.

4. Electronics Integration: Once the display panel is integrated, other electronic components such as processors, memory modules, control boards, and power supplies are connected and configured. This involves intricate wiring and assembly to ensure proper functionality and compatibility between components. Advanced TVs, such as smart TVs, may also include additional features like internet connectivity, HDMI ports, USB ports, and wireless connectivity modules, which are integrated during this stage.

5. Quality Control and Testing: Throughout the manufacturing process, rigorous quality control measures are implemented to ensure that each TV meets predefined standards of performance, reliability, and safety. This involves both automated and manual inspection of components, assemblies, and finished products for defects, imperfections, or malfunctions. Testing procedures may include visual inspection, functional testing, stress testing, and compliance testing to ensure adherence to regulatory standards and industry specifications.

6. Packaging and Shipping: Once the TVs pass quality control checks, they are carefully packaged to protect them from damage during transit. Packaging materials may include cardboard boxes, foam padding, plastic wraps, and protective inserts to safeguard the TV during handling and shipping. Finished products are then labeled, palletized, and prepared for distribution to retailers, wholesalers, or end customers.

7. After-Sales Support: After the TVs are shipped, manufacturers provide various forms of after-sales support to customers, including warranties, technical assistance, and repair services.

This ensures customer satisfaction and helps address any issues or concerns that may arise post-purchase.

Overall, the manufacturing process of televisions involves a combination of precision engineering, advanced technology, and rigorous quality control to produce high-quality, reliable products that meet the demands of consumers worldwide. Each stage of the process is carefully orchestrated to ensure efficiency, consistency, and adherence to industry standards.

COMPONENTS AND ASSEMBLY TECHNIQUES

The manufacturing of televisions (TVs) involves the integration of various components and the application of specific assembly techniques to produce functional and high-quality devices. Here are the fundamentals of TV manufacturing components and assembly techniques:

1. Display Panels:

   - LCD (Liquid Crystal Display): LCD panels consist of a layer of liquid crystal material sandwiched between two glass plates. They rely on backlighting (usually LED) to illuminate the liquid crystals and produce images.

   - LED (Light-Emitting Diode): LED panels utilize an array of light-emitting diodes as the light source. These panels can be either edge-lit or direct-lit, depending on the placement of the LEDs.

   - OLED (Organic Light-Emitting Diode): OLED panels use organic compounds that emit light when an electric current is applied. Unlike LCDs, OLEDs do not require a separate backlight, allowing for thinner and more flexible displays.

   - QLED (Quantum Dot Light Emitting Diode): QLED panels incorporate quantum dot technology to enhance color reproduction and brightness levels. They utilize LED backlighting and quantum dots to produce vibrant and lifelike images.

2. Circuit Boards and Electronics:

- Mainboard (Motherboard): The mainboard serves as the central control unit of the TV, housing the processor (CPU), memory modules, and other essential components.

- Power Supply Board: The power supply board regulates and distributes electrical power to the various components of the TV.

- Control Boards: Control boards manage the functionality of specific features and functions, such as audio processing, input/output interfaces, and smart TV capabilities.

- Connectivity Modules: These modules provide connectivity options such as HDMI, USB, Ethernet, Wi-Fi, and Bluetooth, enabling users to connect external devices and access online content.

3. Audio Components:

- Speakers: Speakers produce sound output and are typically integrated into the TV chassis. Some TVs feature additional audio enhancement technologies such as surround sound, virtual audio processing, and built-in subwoofers.

- Audio Amplifiers: Amplifiers amplify the audio signals generated by the TV's audio processing circuitry, providing sufficient power to drive the speakers.

4. Chassis and Casings:

- Chassis: The chassis serves as the structural frame of the TV, providing support and housing for internal components. It is usually made of metal or plastic and is designed to accommodate the display panel, circuit boards, and other hardware.

- Bezel and Frame: The bezel is the border surrounding the display panel, while the frame provides additional structural support and aesthetic appeal. These components are typically made of plastic or metal and come in various colors and finishes.

5. Assembly Techniques:

- Surface Mount Technology (SMT): Surface mount technology is commonly used for mounting electronic components onto circuit boards. It involves placing components directly onto the surface of the board and soldering them in place using solder paste and reflow soldering techniques.

- Through-Hole Technology (THT): Through-hole technology involves inserting component leads through holes in the circuit board and soldering them to pads on the opposite side. While less common than SMT, THT is still used for certain components that require stronger mechanical connections.

- Adhesive Bonding: Adhesive bonding techniques are used to secure components, panels, and casings together. Adhesives such as epoxy, acrylic, and silicone are applied to join surfaces, providing structural integrity and vibration damping.

6. Quality Control and Testing:
- Various quality control measures are implemented throughout the manufacturing process to ensure that each TV meets predefined standards of performance, reliability, and safety. These may include visual inspection, functional testing, stress testing, and compliance testing to ensure adherence to regulatory standards and industry specifications.

Certainly, here's the continuation:

7. Backlighting and Panel Integration:
- Backlighting: In LCD-based TVs, backlighting is a crucial component that illuminates the liquid crystals to produce images. LED backlighting is the most common method used, either in the form of edge-lit or direct-lit arrays positioned behind the LCD panel. Advanced technologies like local dimming are employed to enhance contrast and energy efficiency.

- Panel Integration: Once the components are prepared, the display panel (LCD, LED, OLED, etc.) is integrated into the TV assembly. This involves carefully aligning the panel within the chassis and connecting it to the control circuitry. Special care is taken to ensure uniformity, alignment accuracy, and proper thermal management to avoid overheating.

8. Smart TV Features Integration:
   - Many modern TVs come with smart features, allowing users to access online content, streaming services, apps, and other interactive functionalities. These features require the integration of additional hardware components such as processors, memory modules, Wi-Fi modules, and software platforms. Smart TVs often include user-friendly interfaces and remote control systems to navigate the various features and services seamlessly.

9. Quality Control and Testing (Continued):
   - Throughout the assembly process, rigorous quality control measures are implemented to ensure that each TV meets strict quality standards. Automated inspection systems, such as computer vision and machine learning algorithms, may be used to detect defects, misalignments, or anomalies in components, assemblies, and finished products. Functional testing ensures that all features and functions operate correctly, including audio and video performance, connectivity, and smart features.

10. Packaging and Distribution:
    - Once the TVs pass quality control checks, they are carefully packaged to protect them from damage during transportation and handling. Packaging materials are chosen to provide adequate cushioning and protection against shocks and vibrations. Finished products are labeled, palletized, and prepared for distribution to retailers, wholesalers, or end customers. Logistics and distribution networks ensure timely delivery and efficient supply chain management.

11. After-Sales Support (Continued):
    - After the TVs are shipped, manufacturers provide various forms of after-sales support to customers. This may include warranties, technical assistance, troubleshooting guides, and

repair services. Customer feedback and satisfaction surveys help manufacturers identify areas for improvement and enhance product quality and service levels.

In summary, the manufacturing process of televisions involves the integration of diverse components, specialized assembly techniques, rigorous quality control measures, and careful attention to detail to produce reliable, high-quality devices that meet the demands of consumers for superior visual and audio experiences. Advanced technologies and continuous innovation drive improvements in performance, features, and efficiency, ensuring that TVs remain at the forefront of entertainment and communication technology.

MACHINE LEARNING APPLICATIONS

Artificial Intelligence (AI) technologies, particularly machine learning, are increasingly being integrated into various aspects of TV manufacturing to improve efficiency, quality, and innovation. Here are some machine learning applications in TV manufacturing:

1. Predictive Maintenance:
   - Machine learning algorithms analyze historical data from sensors embedded in TV components to predict when equipment is likely to fail.
   - By detecting patterns and anomalies in data, predictive maintenance models can identify potential issues before they cause downtime, enabling proactive repair or replacement of components.
   - This approach minimizes unplanned downtime, reduces maintenance costs, and extends the lifespan of equipment.

2. Quality Control and Defect Detection:
   - Computer vision systems powered by machine learning algorithms can automatically inspect TV components and assemblies for defects and anomalies.
   - These systems analyze images and video streams captured by cameras to detect imperfections such as scratches, dents, misalignments, and color inconsistencies.
   - Machine learning models can be trained on large datasets of labeled images to improve accuracy and reliability in defect detection, reducing the need for manual inspection and

increasing production efficiency.

3. Product Customization and Personalization:
- Machine learning algorithms analyze customer data and preferences to recommend personalized TV configurations and features.
- By understanding individual preferences for screen size, resolution, smart features, and connectivity options, manufacturers can tailor product offerings to meet the specific needs of each customer segment.
- This personalized approach enhances customer satisfaction and loyalty, driving sales and revenue growth in competitive markets.

4. Supply Chain Optimization:
- Machine learning algorithms analyze data from various sources, such as sales forecasts, supplier performance metrics, and inventory levels, to optimize supply chain operations.
- These algorithms can predict demand fluctuations, identify potential bottlenecks, and optimize inventory levels to ensure efficient production and distribution of TVs.
- By optimizing supply chain processes, manufacturers can reduce costs, improve delivery times, and enhance overall operational efficiency.

5. Energy Efficiency Optimization:
- Machine learning algorithms analyze data from energy consumption sensors and environmental monitoring systems to optimize energy usage in TV manufacturing facilities.
- These algorithms can identify opportunities for energy savings, such as optimizing equipment usage schedules, adjusting lighting and HVAC systems, and implementing energy-efficient technologies.
- By reducing energy consumption and carbon emissions, manufacturers can lower operating costs, comply with regulatory requirements, and demonstrate corporate social responsibility.

6. Voice and Gesture Recognition:

- Machine learning algorithms power voice and gesture recognition systems embedded in smart TVs, enabling intuitive and hands-free interaction with the device.

- These systems can understand spoken commands and gestures, allowing users to control TV functions, navigate menus, and access content effortlessly.

- By leveraging machine learning models trained on diverse datasets of speech and gesture patterns, manufacturers can deliver seamless and responsive user experiences, enhancing the appeal and usability of their products.

Overall, machine learning applications in TV manufacturing enable manufacturers to improve efficiency, quality, and innovation across the production process, from predictive maintenance and defect detection to supply chain optimization and personalized customer experiences. By harnessing the power of machine learning, manufacturers can stay competitive in the rapidly evolving consumer electronics market and meet the evolving demands of tech-savvy consumers.

COMPUTER VISION FOR QUALITY INSPECTION

Computer vision, a subset of artificial intelligence (AI), plays a significant role in quality inspection within TV manufacturing processes. By leveraging advanced image processing algorithms, computer vision systems can analyze visual data from cameras and sensors to detect defects, anomalies, and deviations from quality standards. Here's how computer vision is applied for quality inspection in TV manufacturing:

1. Automated Defect Detection:
   - Computer vision algorithms analyze images or video streams of TV components and assemblies captured by cameras.
   - By comparing captured images to predefined quality standards and reference images, the system can automatically identify defects such as scratches, dents, discolorations, or misalignments.
   - Machine learning models trained on labeled datasets can improve accuracy and reliability in defect detection, enabling the system to adapt to variations in lighting conditions, surface textures, and defect types.

2. Surface Inspection:
   - Computer vision systems inspect the surfaces of TV panels, casings, and other components for imperfections and irregularities.

- High-resolution cameras capture detailed images of surfaces, enabling the system to detect surface defects such as scratches, smudges, blemishes, or uneven coatings.

- Advanced image processing techniques, including edge detection, texture analysis, and pattern recognition, enhance the system's ability to detect subtle surface defects and anomalies.

3. Alignment and Assembly Verification:

- Computer vision algorithms verify the alignment and assembly of TV components to ensure proper fit and functionality.

- By analyzing images of assembled components, the system can detect misalignments, gaps, or deviations from design specifications.

- This helps ensure that components are correctly positioned and assembled, preventing issues such as display misalignment, connectivity problems, or structural weaknesses.

4. Visual Inspection of Display Panels:

- Computer vision systems inspect display panels (LCD, LED, OLED, etc.) for pixel defects, uniformity issues, and color accuracy.

- By analyzing images captured at various viewing angles and under different lighting conditions, the system can identify dead pixels, stuck pixels, backlight bleeding, and other display abnormalities.

- This ensures that TVs meet stringent quality standards for visual performance and image quality, enhancing customer satisfaction and brand reputation.

5. Quality Control in Production Lines:

- Computer vision systems are integrated into production lines to perform real-time quality control inspections during manufacturing.

- Cameras and sensors are positioned at key stages of the production process to capture images of components and assemblies as they move along the assembly line.

- Automated algorithms analyze captured images and provide immediate feedback to operators or trigger alerts for corrective actions in case of defects or quality issues.

6. Defect Classification and Sorting:

- Computer vision systems classify detected defects based on their type, severity, and location, enabling manufacturers to prioritize corrective actions.

- Defective units may be automatically sorted out for rework or repair, ensuring that only products meeting quality standards are shipped to customers.

- This reduces the risk of product recalls, minimizes waste, and improves overall production efficiency and cost-effectiveness.

In summary, computer vision technologies play a crucial role in quality inspection within TV manufacturing processes, enabling automated defect detection, surface inspection, alignment verification, display panel inspection, real-time quality control, and defect classification. By leveraging advanced image processing algorithms and machine learning techniques, manufacturers can enhance product quality, reduce production costs, and improve customer satisfaction in today's competitive consumer electronics market.

PREDICTIVE MAINTENANCE USING AI

Predictive maintenance using Artificial Intelligence (AI) is a critical application in the TV manufacturing industry, aimed at improving equipment reliability, minimizing downtime, and optimizing maintenance schedules. Here's how predictive maintenance using AI technologies is applied in TV manufacturing:

1. Data Collection and Monitoring:
   - Sensors are installed on critical equipment and machinery throughout the manufacturing facility to collect real-time data on various parameters such as temperature, vibration, pressure, and power consumption.
   - Data from sensors are continuously monitored and transmitted to a central data repository for analysis. This data forms the basis for predictive maintenance algorithms to detect anomalies and predict potential failures.

2. Data Analysis and Machine Learning:
   - AI-powered predictive maintenance algorithms analyze the collected data to identify patterns, trends, and anomalies indicative of impending equipment failures.
   - Machine learning models are trained on historical maintenance records and sensor data to learn the normal operating behavior of equipment and detect deviations from

expected patterns.
- These models can detect subtle changes in equipment conditions that may precede failures, enabling early intervention and preventive maintenance measures.

3. Failure Prediction and Prognostics:
- Predictive maintenance algorithms use machine learning techniques such as regression analysis, anomaly detection, and time-series forecasting to predict when equipment is likely to fail.
- By analyzing trends in sensor data and equipment performance metrics, predictive models can estimate the remaining useful life (RUL) of components and predict the time to failure with a high degree of accuracy.
- Prognostic models provide actionable insights to maintenance teams, allowing them to schedule maintenance activities proactively and minimize disruptions to production operations.

4. Maintenance Planning and Optimization:
- Predictive maintenance algorithms generate maintenance schedules and recommendations based on the predicted health and condition of equipment.
- Maintenance tasks are prioritized based on the criticality of equipment, the severity of potential failures, and the availability of resources.
- Maintenance schedules are optimized to minimize downtime, maximize equipment uptime, and reduce maintenance costs by avoiding unnecessary inspections and repairs.

5. Condition-Based Monitoring and Alerts:
- Predictive maintenance systems provide real-time monitoring of equipment conditions and trigger alerts when abnormalities or anomalies are detected.
- Maintenance teams receive notifications via dashboards, email alerts, or mobile applications, enabling them to take

immediate action to address potential issues.

- Condition-based monitoring allows maintenance teams to intervene before equipment failures occur, preventing costly downtime and production losses.

6. Performance Tracking and Analysis:

- Predictive maintenance systems track the performance of maintenance activities and measure their effectiveness in preventing failures and extending equipment life.

- Key performance indicators (KPIs) such as mean time between failures (MTBF), mean time to repair (MTTR), and overall equipment effectiveness (OEE) are monitored and analyzed to assess the impact of predictive maintenance on production efficiency and equipment reliability.

- Continuous feedback and improvement loops ensure that predictive maintenance algorithms evolve over time to adapt to changing equipment conditions and operational requirements.

In summary, predictive maintenance using AI technologies enables TV manufacturers to monitor equipment health in real-time, predict potential failures, and optimize maintenance schedules to maximize equipment uptime and productivity. By leveraging advanced data analytics and machine learning techniques, manufacturers can reduce maintenance costs, minimize downtime, and improve overall equipment reliability in today's fast-paced manufacturing environment.

ROBOTICS AND AUTOMATION

Robotics and automation powered by Artificial Intelligence (AI) are revolutionizing TV manufacturing processes by enhancing efficiency, precision, and productivity. Here's how robotics and automation are utilized in TV manufacturing:

1. Automated Assembly Lines:
   - Robotics are employed in assembly lines to automate repetitive tasks such as component placement, soldering, and fastening.
   - Automated guided vehicles (AGVs) transport components and sub-assemblies between workstations, optimizing material flow and reducing manual handling.
   - AI-powered robotic arms equipped with vision systems can manipulate and assemble delicate components with high precision and accuracy, ensuring consistency and quality.

2. Pick-and-Place Operations:
   - Robots equipped with suction grippers, mechanical grippers, or vacuum systems are used for pick-and-place operations to handle components and parts during assembly.
   - AI algorithms optimize robot trajectories and gripping strategies to maximize efficiency and minimize cycle times.
   - Vision systems enable robots to identify and locate components accurately, even in cluttered or unstructured environments.

3. Material Handling and Logistics:

- Automated guided vehicles (AGVs) and autonomous mobile robots (AMRs) transport materials, components, and finished products between different areas of the manufacturing facility.

- AI algorithms optimize route planning, scheduling, and navigation to minimize travel times and maximize throughput.

- Robotics enable just-in-time (JIT) delivery of components to assembly lines, reducing inventory holding costs and streamlining production processes.

4. Quality Inspection and Testing:

- Robotics are used in conjunction with computer vision systems for automated quality inspection and testing of TV components and assemblies.

- Robots equipped with cameras and sensors scan components for defects, anomalies, and deviations from quality standards.

- AI algorithms analyze captured images and data to detect defects, classify anomalies, and trigger alerts for corrective action.

5. Packaging and Palletizing:

- Robotics automate packaging and palletizing operations at the end of the assembly line, reducing manual labor and increasing efficiency.

- Robotic arms equipped with grippers or suction cups handle finished products, placing them into packaging containers or onto pallets.

- AI algorithms optimize packing densities, stack heights, and load configurations to maximize space utilization and minimize shipping costs.

6. Maintenance and Servicing:

- Robotics are utilized for predictive maintenance and servicing of manufacturing equipment and machinery.

- Autonomous maintenance robots equipped with sensors and diagnostic tools inspect, monitor, and repair equipment, reducing downtime and maintenance costs.

- AI algorithms analyze equipment performance data and

predict potential failures, enabling proactive maintenance interventions and minimizing unplanned downtime.

7. Human-Robot Collaboration:
- Collaborative robots (cobots) work alongside human operators in TV manufacturing facilities, performing tasks that require dexterity, precision, or physical strength.
- AI-powered cobots adapt their behavior and movements in real-time to ensure safe and efficient collaboration with human workers.
- Cobots enhance productivity, ergonomics, and flexibility on the factory floor, allowing manufacturers to automate a wide range of tasks while retaining human oversight and expertise.

In summary, robotics and automation powered by AI technologies are transforming TV manufacturing processes, enabling manufacturers to achieve higher levels of efficiency, precision, and productivity. By integrating robotics into assembly lines, material handling operations, quality inspection processes, and maintenance activities, manufacturers can optimize production workflows, reduce costs, and deliver high-quality products to market faster.

DATA SOURCES IN TV MANUFACTURING

Data collection and analysis are essential components of modern TV manufacturing processes, enabling manufacturers to monitor equipment performance, optimize production workflows, and ensure product quality. Here are some key data sources in TV manufacturing:

1. Sensor Data:
   - Sensors embedded in manufacturing equipment and machinery collect real-time data on various parameters such as temperature, pressure, vibration, humidity, and power consumption.
   - Sensor data provide insights into the operational status and health of equipment, allowing manufacturers to detect anomalies, predict failures, and optimize maintenance schedules.

2. Production Line Data:
   - Data from production line equipment, including conveyor belts, robotic arms, and assembly stations, provide insights into production rates, cycle times, and throughput.
   - Monitoring production line data helps manufacturers identify bottlenecks, optimize workflow efficiency, and improve overall manufacturing productivity.

3. Quality Control Data:
   - Data from quality control inspections, including visual

inspections, defect detection, and functional testing, provide insights into product quality and compliance with quality standards.

- Analyzing quality control data helps manufacturers identify defects, root causes, and areas for improvement in the manufacturing process.

4. Supply Chain Data:

- Data from supply chain operations, including inventory levels, procurement activities, and supplier performance metrics, provide insights into supply chain efficiency and reliability.

- Monitoring supply chain data helps manufacturers optimize inventory management, minimize stockouts, and ensure timely delivery of components and materials.

5. Maintenance Records:

- Data from maintenance activities, including work orders, service logs, and equipment maintenance history, provide insights into equipment reliability and maintenance requirements.

- Analyzing maintenance records helps manufacturers optimize maintenance schedules, predict equipment failures, and reduce unplanned downtime.

6. Customer Feedback and Warranty Claims:

- Data from customer feedback, warranty claims, and product returns provide insights into product performance, reliability, and customer satisfaction.

- Monitoring customer feedback data helps manufacturers identify product issues, address customer concerns, and improve product quality and design.

7. Environmental Data:

- Data from environmental monitoring systems, including air quality sensors, temperature sensors, and humidity sensors, provide insights into environmental conditions within the manufacturing facility.

- Monitoring environmental data helps manufacturers ensure compliance with regulatory requirements, maintain worker safety, and optimize manufacturing processes.

8. Energy Consumption Data:

- Data from energy meters and monitoring systems provide insights into energy consumption patterns and trends within the manufacturing facility.

- Analyzing energy consumption data helps manufacturers identify opportunities for energy savings, optimize equipment usage, and reduce operating costs.

By collecting and analyzing data from these sources, TV manufacturers can gain valuable insights into their manufacturing processes, equipment performance, product quality, and supply chain operations. This enables manufacturers to optimize production efficiency, reduce costs, and deliver high-quality products to customers.

DATA ACQUISITION METHODS

In TV manufacturing, data acquisition methods play a crucial role in collecting relevant data from various sources throughout the production process. Here are some common data acquisition methods used in TV manufacturing:

1. Sensor Technology:
    - Sensors are widely used in TV manufacturing to collect real-time data on various parameters such as temperature, pressure, vibration, humidity, and power consumption.
    - Different types of sensors, including temperature sensors, pressure sensors, accelerometers, and proximity sensors, are strategically placed on equipment, machinery, and production lines to monitor critical variables.
    - Sensor data are collected continuously and transmitted to data acquisition systems for analysis and interpretation.

2. Embedded Systems:
    - Embedded systems are used to collect data directly from equipment and machinery in TV manufacturing facilities.
    - Microcontrollers, data acquisition modules, and programmable logic controllers (PLCs) are embedded into manufacturing equipment to monitor performance, control operations, and collect sensor data.
    - Embedded systems facilitate real-time data acquisition and control, enabling manufacturers to monitor and optimize production processes efficiently.

3. Supervisory Control and Data Acquisition (SCADA) Systems:
 - SCADA systems are used to collect, monitor, and control data from various sensors and devices in TV manufacturing plants.
 - SCADA software applications gather data from sensors, PLCs, and other industrial devices, providing real-time visualization, analysis, and reporting capabilities.
 - SCADA systems enable manufacturers to monitor equipment performance, track production metrics, and detect anomalies in real-time.

4. Internet of Things (IoT) Devices:
 - IoT devices are increasingly deployed in TV manufacturing to collect data from connected sensors, machines, and devices.
 - IoT sensors embedded in manufacturing equipment and products transmit data wirelessly to centralized data repositories or cloud-based platforms for analysis.
 - IoT devices enable remote monitoring, predictive maintenance, and real-time decision-making in TV manufacturing operations.

5. Machine Vision Systems:
 - Machine vision systems capture visual data from cameras and sensors to monitor and inspect TV components and assemblies.
 - Cameras and imaging sensors are integrated into production lines and inspection stations to capture images and videos of products for quality control and defect detection.
 - Machine vision systems use image processing algorithms to analyze visual data, detect defects, and perform automated inspection tasks.

6. Data Logging and Recording:
 - Data logging systems are used to record and store data from sensors, equipment, and processes in TV manufacturing plants.
 - Data loggers, data acquisition cards, and data acquisition units capture sensor data at predefined intervals and store it in

digital format for analysis and reporting.

- Data logging systems facilitate historical data analysis, trend monitoring, and performance tracking in TV manufacturing processes.

7. Manual Data Entry and Reporting:

- In some cases, data may be collected manually through direct observation, measurements, or manual input by operators.

- Operators record data using paper-based forms, electronic spreadsheets, or data entry interfaces to document production metrics, quality inspection results, and maintenance activities.

- Manual data entry methods are often supplemented with automated data acquisition systems to ensure accuracy and completeness of data records.

By utilizing these data acquisition methods, TV manufacturers can collect, monitor, and analyze data from various sources to optimize production processes, improve product quality, and enhance overall operational efficiency.

DATA PREPROCESSING AND CLEANING

In TV manufacturing, as in any manufacturing process, data preprocessing and cleaning are crucial steps in preparing raw data for analysis. Here's how data preprocessing and cleaning are typically conducted in TV manufacturing:

1. Data Collection:
   - Raw data is collected from various sources such as sensors, production equipment, quality control systems, and environmental monitoring devices.
   - Data may include measurements of temperature, pressure, vibration, humidity, power consumption, production metrics, quality inspection results, and maintenance records.

2. Data Validation:
   - The first step in data preprocessing is to validate the collected data to ensure its accuracy, completeness, and consistency.
   - Data validation involves checking for missing values, outliers, errors, and inconsistencies in the dataset.
   - Invalid or unreliable data points are identified and flagged for further investigation or correction.

3. Data Cleaning:
   - Data cleaning involves removing or correcting errors, inconsistencies, and outliers in the dataset to improve data quality.

- Common data cleaning techniques include:
- Handling missing values: Missing data points are imputed or interpolated using appropriate methods such as mean imputation, median imputation, or predictive modeling.
- Outlier detection and removal: Outliers, which are data points that deviate significantly from the rest of the dataset, are identified using statistical methods or machine learning algorithms and either corrected or removed.
- Data normalization and scaling: Numeric data features are normalized or scaled to a common range to ensure uniformity and comparability across different variables.
- Data deduplication: Duplicate records or observations in the dataset are identified and eliminated to avoid redundancy and ensure data integrity.

4. Feature Engineering:
- Feature engineering involves transforming and engineering raw data into informative features that are suitable for analysis and modeling.
- This may include creating new features, aggregating existing features, encoding categorical variables, and extracting relevant information from raw data.
- Feature engineering techniques help improve the performance of machine learning models and enhance the interpretability of analysis results.

5. Data Integration:
- In TV manufacturing, data from multiple sources and sources may need to be integrated into a single dataset for analysis.
- Data integration involves merging, joining, or combining datasets from different sources while ensuring data consistency and alignment.
- Integration may require data transformation, standardization, and normalization to harmonize data structures and formats.

6. Data Transformation:

- Data transformation involves converting raw data into a format that is suitable for analysis and modeling.
- This may include transforming categorical variables into numerical representations, encoding date and time variables, and converting text data into numerical features using techniques such as one-hot encoding or word embedding.

7. Data Sampling and Splitting:

- Depending on the analysis objectives, the dataset may be sampled or split into training, validation, and testing sets.
- Sampling techniques such as random sampling, stratified sampling, or oversampling/undersampling may be used to create representative subsets of the data for analysis.
- The dataset is typically split into training data for model training, validation data for model tuning, and testing data for model evaluation.

8. Data Imbalance Handling:

- In cases where the dataset is imbalanced, with unequal distribution of classes or categories, data preprocessing techniques such as oversampling, undersampling, or synthetic data generation may be applied to balance the dataset.

9. Data Quality Assurance:

- Finally, data quality assurance checks are performed to ensure that the preprocessed data meets the desired quality standards and is ready for analysis.
- Quality assurance measures include verifying data consistency, accuracy, and reliability, as well as documenting data preprocessing steps for reproducibility and transparency.

By conducting thorough data preprocessing and cleaning, TV manufacturers can ensure that the data used for analysis and decision-making is accurate, reliable, and representative of the underlying manufacturing processes. This, in turn, enables more effective analysis, modeling, and optimization of production processes, leading to improved product quality, efficiency, and cost-effectiveness.

STATISTICAL ANALYSIS FOR PROCESS OPTIMIZATION

Statistical analysis plays a crucial role in process optimization in TV manufacturing, allowing manufacturers to identify inefficiencies, improve quality, and enhance overall performance. Here's how statistical analysis is applied for process optimization in TV manufacturing:

1. Descriptive Statistics:
   - Descriptive statistics provide a summary of key metrics and characteristics of the manufacturing process.
   - Measures such as mean, median, standard deviation, range, and percentiles are used to describe the central tendency, dispersion, and distribution of process variables such as temperature, pressure, and production rates.
   - Descriptive statistics help manufacturers gain insights into the current state of the manufacturing process and identify areas for improvement.

2. Control Charts:
   - Control charts are used to monitor process stability and detect variations in process performance over time.
   - Statistical control limits, such as upper and lower control limits, are calculated based on historical data and process

specifications.

- Control charts help manufacturers identify abnormal variations, trends, and patterns in process data, allowing them to take corrective actions to maintain process stability and consistency.

3. Process Capability Analysis:

- Process capability analysis assesses the ability of the manufacturing process to meet customer requirements and specifications.

- Metrics such as process capability indices (e.g., Cp, Cpk) are used to quantify the capability of the process to produce parts within specified tolerances.

- Process capability analysis helps manufacturers identify process deficiencies, reduce variation, and improve product quality by optimizing process parameters and settings.

4. Experimental Design:

- Experimental design, including techniques such as design of experiments (DOE) and factorial experiments, is used to systematically investigate the effects of process variables on product quality and performance.

- Experiments are designed to manipulate process variables (factors) at different levels and measure their impact on key outcomes (responses) such as defect rates, cycle times, and yield.

- Statistical analysis of experimental data helps manufacturers identify significant factors, optimize process settings, and achieve desired outcomes with minimal resources and time.

5. Regression Analysis:

- Regression analysis is used to model the relationship between input variables (predictors) and output variables (responses) in the manufacturing process.

- Multiple regression, logistic regression, and other regression techniques are applied to identify influential factors, quantify their effects, and predict process outcomes.

- Regression analysis helps manufacturers understand the underlying relationships between process parameters and performance metrics, guiding decision-making and process optimization efforts.

6. Statistical Process Control (SPC):
- Statistical process control (SPC) techniques, such as control charts and capability analysis, are used to monitor and manage process variability in real-time.
- SPC helps manufacturers detect and correct process deviations, minimize defects, and maintain process stability and consistency.
- By implementing SPC, manufacturers can achieve tighter control over critical process parameters and improve product quality and reliability.

7. Root Cause Analysis:
- Statistical techniques, such as Pareto analysis, fishbone diagrams, and hypothesis testing, are used to identify root causes of process issues and quality problems.
- Root cause analysis helps manufacturers pinpoint underlying factors contributing to process variability, defects, and non-conformities.
- By addressing root causes systematically, manufacturers can implement targeted corrective actions to eliminate process inefficiencies and improve overall process performance.

8. Statistical Modeling and Simulation:
- Statistical modeling and simulation techniques, including simulation software and predictive analytics, are used to predict process behavior and optimize process parameters.
- Modeling approaches such as Monte Carlo simulation, discrete event simulation, and agent-based modeling enable manufacturers to evaluate "what-if" scenarios, optimize resource allocation, and minimize risks.
- Statistical modeling and simulation provide valuable insights into complex manufacturing processes, allowing

manufacturers to optimize production schedules, reduce costs, and improve throughput.

By applying statistical analysis techniques for process optimization, TV manufacturers can enhance product quality, increase production efficiency, and achieve competitive advantages in the marketplace. Through continuous monitoring, analysis, and improvement of manufacturing processes, manufacturers can adapt to changing customer demands, technological advancements, and market dynamics, ensuring long-term success and sustainability.

TRADITIONAL VS. AI-BASED QUALITY CONTROL METHODS

Traditional quality control methods and AI-based quality control methods each have their strengths and weaknesses. Here's a comparison of the two approaches in the context of TV manufacturing:

1. Traditional Quality Control Methods:

Strengths:
- Proven Reliability: Traditional quality control methods, such as manual inspection by human operators, have been used for decades and are well-established in manufacturing processes.
- Flexibility: Human inspectors can adapt to changes in product specifications and visual inspection criteria more easily than automated systems.
- Domain Expertise: Skilled inspectors possess domain knowledge and experience that enable them to detect subtle defects and anomalies that may be challenging for automated systems to identify.

Weaknesses:
- Subjectivity: Human inspection is inherently subjective and may vary between inspectors, leading to inconsistent results and quality issues.
- Labor Intensive: Manual inspection processes require significant labor resources and can be time-consuming,

especially for large-scale manufacturing operations.

- Limited Scalability: Traditional quality control methods may struggle to keep up with the pace of modern manufacturing, particularly in high-volume production environments.

2. AI-based Quality Control Methods:

Strengths:

- High Accuracy: AI-based systems, such as computer vision algorithms, can analyze large volumes of data quickly and accurately, detecting defects with high precision and reliability.
- Consistency: AI-based systems provide consistent results and do not suffer from fatigue or variability like human inspectors.
- Scalability: Once trained, AI-based systems can be deployed at scale across multiple production lines or facilities, enabling efficient quality control in high-volume manufacturing environments.
- Adaptability: AI algorithms can be trained to recognize various types of defects and adapt to changes in product designs or manufacturing processes.

Weaknesses:

- Initial Setup Cost: Implementing AI-based quality control systems may require significant upfront investment in technology, training, and infrastructure.
- Data Dependency: AI algorithms rely on large volumes of labeled training data to learn and generalize patterns effectively. Obtaining and annotating training data can be time-consuming and costly.
- Complexity: Developing and deploying AI-based quality control systems requires specialized expertise in machine learning, computer vision, and data science, which may not be readily available within manufacturing organizations.

In summary, while traditional quality control methods offer reliability and flexibility, they may struggle to meet the demands of modern manufacturing in terms of scalability and efficiency. AI-based quality control methods, on the other hand, provide high accuracy, consistency, and scalability but require initial investment and expertise in AI technologies. Ultimately, a combination of both traditional and AI-based approaches may offer the best balance of reliability, efficiency, and adaptability in TV manufacturing quality control.

IMPLEMENTING COMPUTER VISION FOR DEFECT DETECTION

Implementing computer vision for defect detection in TV manufacturing involves several key steps:

1. Data Collection:
  - Collect a large dataset of images or videos of TV components and assemblies, including both defect-free samples and samples with various types of defects.
  - Ensure that the dataset covers a wide range of defect types, sizes, and orientations to train a robust defect detection model.

2. Data Preprocessing:
  - Preprocess the collected data to standardize image sizes, resolutions, and formats.
  - Augment the dataset by applying transformations such as rotation, scaling, cropping, and flipping to increase variability and improve model generalization.

3. Annotation and Labeling:
  - Annotate and label the images in the dataset to indicate the presence and location of defects.
  - Use annotation tools to draw bounding boxes, polygons, or masks around defects, specifying the type and severity of each

defect.

4. Model Selection:

- Choose a suitable computer vision model architecture for defect detection, such as convolutional neural networks (CNNs) or deep learning-based object detection frameworks like YOLO (You Only Look Once) or Faster R-CNN (Region-based Convolutional Neural Network).

- Consider factors such as model complexity, performance, and computational efficiency when selecting the model architecture.

5. Model Training:

- Split the annotated dataset into training, validation, and testing sets.

- Train the selected computer vision model on the training data using supervised learning techniques.

- Fine-tune the model parameters and hyperparameters to optimize performance on the validation set.

- Monitor the model's performance metrics, such as accuracy, precision, recall, and F1 score, during training to ensure convergence and avoid overfitting.

6. Model Evaluation:

- Evaluate the trained model's performance on the testing dataset using metrics such as precision, recall, F1 score, and accuracy.

- Use confusion matrices and ROC curves to analyze the model's classification performance and identify areas for improvement.

7. Deployment and Integration:

- Deploy the trained defect detection model to the production environment, either on-premises or in the cloud.

- Integrate the model with the manufacturing process by connecting it to cameras or sensors positioned along the production line.

- Develop software interfaces and APIs to communicate between the defect detection system and other manufacturing systems, such as quality control software or robotic arms.

8. Validation and Testing:
- Validate the deployed defect detection system in real-world production conditions to ensure its accuracy, reliability, and robustness.
- Conduct rigorous testing and validation procedures to verify that the system can accurately detect defects under various lighting conditions, angles, and orientations.

9. Continuous Improvement:
- Monitor the performance of the defect detection system over time and collect feedback from operators and quality control personnel.
- Continuously update and improve the model based on new data, feedback, and evolving manufacturing requirements.
- Implement feedback loops and mechanisms for retraining the model periodically to adapt to changes in defect types or manufacturing processes.

By following these steps, manufacturers can effectively implement computer vision for defect detection in TV manufacturing, improving product quality, reducing defects, and enhancing overall manufacturing efficiency.

REAL-TIME MONITORING AND FEEDBACK LOOPS

Real-time monitoring and feedback loops are essential components of quality control and inspection processes in TV manufacturing. Here's how they are implemented:

1. Sensor Integration:
   - Install sensors at critical points along the production line to collect real-time data on key process variables such as temperature, pressure, vibration, and humidity.
   - Use sensors with high sampling rates and precision to capture data at regular intervals and monitor process conditions continuously.

2. Data Acquisition and Processing:
   - Collect sensor data in real-time and transmit it to a centralized data acquisition system or a cloud-based platform.
   - Process and analyze the incoming data streams using algorithms and models to monitor process performance and detect deviations from quality standards.

3. Real-time Monitoring:
   - Implement real-time monitoring dashboards and visualization tools to display key performance indicators (KPIs), process variables, and quality metrics.
   - Provide operators and supervisors with real-time insights into production status, equipment health, and product quality,

allowing them to monitor process performance and intervene promptly when issues arise.

4. Alerting and Notifications:
- Set up automated alerting systems to notify operators and managers of abnormal conditions, out-of-spec measurements, or quality deviations in real-time.
- Trigger alerts via email, SMS, or mobile notifications to ensure that relevant personnel can take immediate corrective actions to address quality issues.

5. Feedback Loops:
- Establish feedback loops between real-time monitoring systems and production equipment to enable closed-loop control and automatic adjustments.
- Use feedback mechanisms to dynamically regulate process parameters, equipment settings, and material flows in response to changing production conditions or quality requirements.

6. Root Cause Analysis:
- Integrate root cause analysis tools and techniques into the real-time monitoring system to identify underlying factors contributing to quality deviations or process anomalies.
- Conduct root cause analysis in real-time to diagnose the root causes of quality issues and implement corrective actions effectively.

7. Continuous Improvement:
- Implement continuous improvement initiatives based on insights gained from real-time monitoring and feedback loops.
- Analyze historical data and performance trends to identify patterns, optimize process parameters, and prevent recurring quality issues.

8. Operator Training and Empowerment:
- Provide operators with training and support to interpret real-time monitoring data effectively and make informed decisions.

- Empower operators to take ownership of quality control and inspection processes by giving them access to real-time data, decision support tools, and training on problem-solving techniques.

By implementing real-time monitoring and feedback loops in TV manufacturing, manufacturers can enhance quality control and inspection processes, improve product quality, and optimize production efficiency. Real-time insights enable timely interventions, proactive problem-solving, and continuous improvement, ensuring that quality standards are consistently met and maintained throughout the manufacturing process.

IMPORTANCE OF PREDICTIVE MAINTENANCE

Predictive maintenance is a proactive maintenance strategy that uses data analytics, machine learning, and condition monitoring to predict equipment failures before they occur. Here are some key reasons why predictive maintenance is important in the context of TV manufacturing:

1. Minimizing Downtime: Predictive maintenance helps minimize unplanned downtime by identifying potential equipment failures in advance. By proactively addressing issues before they lead to breakdowns, manufacturers can avoid costly production stoppages and maintain smooth operations.

2. Reducing Maintenance Costs: Predictive maintenance optimizes maintenance schedules and resource allocation by focusing on equipment that actually needs attention. By performing maintenance activities only when necessary, manufacturers can reduce unnecessary maintenance costs and extend the lifespan of equipment.

3. Improving Equipment Reliability: By identifying and addressing potential failure modes early, predictive maintenance improves equipment reliability and uptime. This leads to more consistent production output and helps meet customer demand without interruptions.

4. Enhancing Product Quality: Equipment failures can lead to defects in TV manufacturing, resulting in quality issues and rework. Predictive maintenance helps prevent equipment failures that could impact product quality, ensuring that TVs meet quality standards and customer expectations.

5. Optimizing Spare Parts Inventory: Predictive maintenance allows manufacturers to better manage spare parts inventory by predicting when parts will need replacement. This helps reduce inventory costs and avoids the risk of stockouts or overstocking.

6. Increasing Safety: Equipment failures can pose safety risks to workers in TV manufacturing facilities. Predictive maintenance helps mitigate these risks by preventing unexpected breakdowns and ensuring that equipment operates safely and reliably.

7. Supporting Lean Manufacturing: Predictive maintenance aligns with principles of lean manufacturing by eliminating waste and improving overall equipment effectiveness (OEE). By optimizing maintenance activities and reducing downtime, manufacturers can achieve higher levels of efficiency and productivity.

8. Enabling Data-Driven Decision Making: Predictive maintenance relies on data analytics and machine learning algorithms to analyze equipment condition and predict failures. This data-driven approach enables manufacturers to make informed decisions about maintenance priorities, resource allocation, and process optimization.

Overall, predictive maintenance is important in TV manufacturing because it helps manufacturers maximize equipment uptime, minimize costs, improve product quality, and enhance overall operational efficiency. By leveraging predictive maintenance technologies and methodologies, manufacturers can stay competitive in the fast-paced consumer electronics industry and meet the demands of today's market.

AI ALGORITHMS FOR PREDICTING EQUIPMENT FAILURES

Several AI algorithms can be employed for predicting equipment failures in TV manufacturing. Here are some commonly used algorithms:

1. Machine Learning (ML) Algorithms:

- Random Forest: Random Forest is an ensemble learning algorithm that combines multiple decision trees to make predictions. It is robust and can handle large datasets with high dimensionality, making it suitable for predicting equipment failures based on various sensor data and process parameters.

- Gradient Boosting Machines (GBM): GBM is another ensemble learning technique that builds multiple weak learners sequentially to improve prediction accuracy. It is effective for detecting complex patterns in data and can be applied to predict equipment failures based on historical maintenance records and sensor data.

- Support Vector Machines (SVM): SVM is a supervised learning algorithm that is used for classification and regression tasks. It works well for predicting equipment failures by identifying patterns in sensor data and detecting anomalies indicative of potential failures.

- Neural Networks: Neural networks, especially deep learning architectures such as convolutional neural networks (CNNs) and recurrent neural networks (RNNs), can learn complex relationships in sensor data and time-series data. They are effective for predicting equipment failures based on sequential sensor readings and historical maintenance logs.

2. Anomaly Detection Algorithms:
   - Isolation Forest: Isolation Forest is an unsupervised learning algorithm that isolates anomalies by randomly partitioning data points into subsets. It is suitable for detecting outliers and anomalies in sensor data that may indicate equipment failures.
   - One-Class Support Vector Machines (OCSVM): OCSVM is a type of SVM that is trained on only one class of data (normal instances) and then used to detect outliers or anomalies. It can be applied for predicting equipment failures by identifying deviations from normal operating conditions.
   - Autoencoders: Autoencoders are neural network architectures used for unsupervised learning and dimensionality reduction. They can learn a compressed representation of sensor data and reconstruct normal patterns. Deviations from the reconstructed data can indicate anomalies or equipment failures.

3. Time-Series Forecasting Algorithms:
   - ARIMA (AutoRegressive Integrated Moving Average): ARIMA is a popular time-series forecasting algorithm that models the temporal dependence and seasonality in data. It can be used to predict future equipment failures based on historical sensor readings and maintenance logs.
   - Long Short-Term Memory (LSTM): LSTM is a type of recurrent neural network (RNN) that is well-suited for modeling sequential data with long-term dependencies. It can be applied for time-series forecasting of equipment failures based on sensor data collected over time.

4. Survival Analysis:
   - Cox Proportional Hazards Model: Cox Proportional Hazards Model is a statistical technique used for survival analysis, which estimates the probability of failure over time. It can be applied

to predict equipment failures by analyzing the time until failure based on historical maintenance records and sensor data.

These AI algorithms can be trained on historical data, including sensor readings, maintenance logs, and failure records, to learn patterns and relationships that indicate impending equipment failures. By deploying predictive maintenance systems based on these algorithms, TV manufacturers can identify potential failures in advance, minimize downtime, and optimize maintenance schedules.

IMPLEMENTATING PREDICTIVE MAINTENANCE AND CASE STUDIES

Implementing predictive maintenance (PdM) involves several key strategies and methodologies. Here are some common implementation strategies along with case studies illustrating their application in various industries, including TV manufacturing:

1. Data Collection and Integration:

- Strategy: Collect and integrate data from sensors, equipment, and other sources to build a comprehensive dataset for predictive maintenance analysis.

- Case Study: General Electric (GE) implemented a predictive maintenance system called Predix, which collects data from sensors embedded in industrial equipment such as turbines and generators. By analyzing this data using machine learning algorithms, GE can predict equipment failures and schedule maintenance proactively, reducing downtime and increasing operational efficiency.

2. Condition Monitoring and Sensor Deployment:

- Strategy: Deploy sensors and monitoring devices to collect real-time data on equipment health and performance.

- Case Study: Rolls-Royce uses condition monitoring systems

to collect data from aircraft engines during flight operations. By analyzing this data, Rolls-Royce can detect anomalies and signs of wear or damage in engine components, allowing for timely maintenance interventions and reducing the risk of in-flight failures.

3. Predictive Analytics and Machine Learning:

- Strategy: Apply predictive analytics and machine learning algorithms to analyze historical data and predict equipment failures.

- Case Study: Rio Tinto, a global mining company, implemented a predictive maintenance system for its fleet of autonomous trucks used in mining operations. By analyzing telemetry data from the trucks, Rio Tinto can predict component failures and schedule maintenance proactively, optimizing truck availability and reducing maintenance costs.

4. Integration with Enterprise Systems:

- Strategy: Integrate predictive maintenance systems with enterprise asset management (EAM) and enterprise resource planning (ERP) systems to streamline maintenance workflows and optimize resource allocation.

- Case Study: Siemens implemented a predictive maintenance solution for its wind turbines, integrating the system with its EAM software. By automatically generating work orders and scheduling maintenance tasks based on predictive analytics, Siemens can optimize maintenance schedules and reduce downtime for wind turbine operations.

5. Continuous Improvement and Optimization:

- Strategy: Continuously monitor and evaluate the performance of predictive maintenance systems, and iterate on the algorithms and methodologies to improve accuracy and reliability.

- Case Study: SKF, a global manufacturer of bearings and other industrial components, implemented a predictive maintenance system for its rotating equipment. By continuously refining its predictive models and incorporating feedback from maintenance technicians, SKF has achieved significant improvements in equipment uptime and reliability across its manufacturing facilities.

6. Change Management and Training:

   - Strategy: Provide training and support to maintenance technicians and operators to ensure successful adoption and implementation of predictive maintenance practices.

   - Case Study: Boeing implemented a predictive maintenance system for its fleet of commercial aircraft. Boeing provided comprehensive training programs for maintenance technicians and flight crews to familiarize them with the new predictive maintenance tools and processes, facilitating smooth adoption and integration into existing maintenance workflows.

By adopting these implementation strategies and leveraging predictive maintenance technologies, TV manufacturers can optimize equipment uptime, reduce maintenance costs, and improve overall operational efficiency. Additionally, these case studies highlight how predictive maintenance can be successfully applied across various industries to achieve tangible business benefits and competitive advantages.

AI-DRIVEN SUPPLY CHAIN MANAGEMENT

AI-driven supply chain management leverages artificial intelligence (AI) technologies to optimize various aspects of the supply chain, from demand forecasting to inventory management and logistics. Here are some key components and benefits of AI-driven supply chain management:

1. Demand Forecasting:
   - AI algorithms analyze historical sales data, market trends, and external factors (e.g., weather, economic indicators) to generate accurate demand forecasts.
   - By predicting demand more accurately, companies can optimize inventory levels, reduce stockouts, and improve customer satisfaction.

2. Inventory Optimization:
   - AI-driven inventory optimization algorithms continuously analyze demand patterns, lead times, and supply chain constraints to determine optimal inventory levels.
   - Dynamic inventory management helps companies minimize excess inventory while ensuring product availability and reducing carrying costs.

3. Supplier Management:
   - AI-powered supplier management systems analyze supplier performance data, market conditions, and risk factors to identify opportunities for cost savings and risk mitigation.
   - Predictive analytics help companies anticipate supplier

disruptions and proactively manage supplier relationships to maintain continuity in the supply chain.

4. Logistics and Transportation:

- AI algorithms optimize transportation routes, modes, and carriers to minimize costs, reduce transit times, and improve delivery reliability.

- Machine learning models analyze historical shipment data, traffic patterns, and real-time information to optimize delivery schedules and route planning.

5. Warehouse Management:

- AI-driven warehouse management systems (WMS) optimize layout design, inventory placement, and order picking processes to maximize efficiency and throughput.

- Robotics and automation technologies powered by AI enhance warehouse operations by automating repetitive tasks, reducing labor costs, and improving accuracy.

6. Risk Management:

- AI-based risk management tools analyze supply chain data, market trends, and external events to identify potential risks and vulnerabilities.

- Predictive analytics help companies assess and mitigate risks related to supplier disruptions, natural disasters, geopolitical events, and other factors that could impact supply chain operations.

7. Predictive Maintenance:

- AI-driven predictive maintenance systems analyze equipment sensor data, historical maintenance records, and failure patterns to predict equipment failures and schedule maintenance proactively.

- By reducing unplanned downtime and optimizing maintenance schedules, companies can improve equipment reliability and minimize disruptions in the supply chain.

8. Continuous Improvement:

- AI-powered analytics provide insights into supply chain performance, identify areas for improvement, and support data-driven decision-making.
- Continuous monitoring and optimization enable companies to adapt to changing market conditions, customer preferences, and business requirements, ensuring resilience and agility in the supply chain.

Overall, AI-driven supply chain management offers significant benefits, including improved efficiency, reduced costs, enhanced visibility, and greater agility. By leveraging AI technologies to optimize supply chain processes, companies can gain a competitive edge in today's dynamic and increasingly complex business environment.

DEMAND FORECASTING USING MACHINE LEARNING

Demand forecasting using machine learning involves using historical data and other relevant factors to predict future demand for products or services. Here's how it works and some key considerations:

1. Data Collection:
   - Gather historical sales data, including information on product sales, customer orders, and market trends. Additional data sources such as marketing campaigns, promotions, and economic indicators can also be useful.
   - Ensure data quality and consistency by cleaning and preprocessing the data to remove outliers, handle missing values, and normalize the data.

2. Feature Selection and Engineering:
   - Identify relevant features (variables) that may influence demand, such as time of year, pricing, promotions, and external factors like weather or economic conditions.
   - Engineer new features if necessary, such as lagged variables (e.g., previous sales) or seasonal indicators, to capture patterns and trends in the data.

3. Model Selection:
   - Choose appropriate machine learning models for demand forecasting, such as:

- Time-series forecasting models: Models like ARIMA, SARIMA, or Prophet are commonly used for forecasting time-series data.

- Regression models: Linear regression, decision trees, and ensemble methods like random forests or gradient boosting can be effective for demand prediction when considering multiple factors.

- Neural networks: Deep learning architectures like recurrent neural networks (RNNs) or long short-term memory networks (LSTMs) can capture complex temporal dependencies in the data.

4. Model Training:
  - Split the historical data into training and validation sets.
  - Train the selected machine learning models using the training data, tuning hyperparameters and optimizing model performance on the validation set.
  - Validate the model's performance using metrics such as mean absolute error (MAE), mean squared error (MSE), or root mean squared error (RMSE).

5. Model Evaluation:
  - Evaluate the trained model's performance on a holdout test dataset to assess its accuracy and generalization capability.
  - Compare the forecasted demand values with actual demand to measure the model's accuracy and identify areas for improvement.

6. Deployment and Monitoring:
  - Deploy the trained demand forecasting model into production, integrating it into the supply chain management system or decision-making processes.
  - Monitor the model's performance over time, retraining it periodically with updated data to adapt to changing market conditions and demand patterns.
  - Implement feedback mechanisms to capture user feedback and incorporate it into future model iterations.

7. Integration with Supply Chain Planning:
   - Integrate the demand forecasting model with supply chain planning processes to optimize inventory management, production scheduling, and procurement decisions.
   - Use the forecasted demand values to inform inventory replenishment strategies, allocate resources effectively, and optimize supply chain operations.

8. Continuous Improvement:
   - Continuously evaluate and refine the demand forecasting model based on feedback, new data, and changing business requirements.
   - Experiment with different feature combinations, model architectures, and algorithms to improve forecast accuracy and robustness over time.

By leveraging machine learning for demand forecasting, companies can improve inventory management, reduce stockouts, and enhance overall supply chain efficiency. Additionally, accurate demand predictions enable businesses to optimize production planning, allocate resources effectively, and meet customer demand more efficiently.

INVENTORY MANAGEMENT AND OPTIMIZATION

Inventory management and optimization are critical components of supply chain optimization. Here's a comprehensive approach to inventory management using various strategies:

1. Demand Forecasting:
   - Utilize demand forecasting techniques, including statistical methods and machine learning algorithms, to predict future demand accurately.
   - Forecast demand at different levels (e.g., SKU, product category, region) to capture variations and trends in customer demand patterns.
   - Incorporate factors such as seasonality, promotions, market trends, and historical sales data into the forecasting models to improve accuracy.

2. Inventory Classification:
   - Classify inventory items based on their value, demand variability, and criticality using methods such as ABC analysis or XYZ analysis.
   - Prioritize inventory management efforts and allocate resources based on the classification to focus on high-value or critical items while optimizing inventory levels for low-value or non-critical items.

3. Safety Stock Management:
- Determine safety stock levels based on demand variability, lead times, service level targets, and supply chain uncertainties.
- Employ statistical methods such as the reorder point formula, inventory simulation, or probabilistic models to calculate safety stock levels and buffer inventory against demand fluctuations and supply disruptions.

4. Reorder Point and Order Quantity Optimization:
- Calculate optimal reorder points and order quantities using inventory optimization models like Economic Order Quantity (EOQ), reorder point formula with service level targets, or stochastic inventory models.
- Consider factors such as carrying costs, ordering costs, lead times, and stockout costs to determine the most cost-effective reorder points and order quantities.

5. Inventory Policies and Strategies:
- Implement inventory policies and strategies tailored to specific inventory characteristics and business objectives, such as just-in-time (JIT), lean inventory, or vendor-managed inventory (VMI).
- Leverage technology and automation solutions, such as barcode scanning, RFID, and inventory management software, to streamline inventory processes and improve visibility and control.

6. Supply Chain Collaboration and Coordination:
- Collaborate with suppliers, distributors, and other supply chain partners to share information, synchronize inventory levels, and align inventory replenishment schedules.
- Implement collaborative planning, forecasting, and replenishment (CPFR) initiatives to improve supply chain visibility, reduce lead times, and minimize stockouts and excess inventory.

7. Continuous Monitoring and Optimization:

- Monitor inventory performance metrics such as inventory turnover, stockout rates, fill rates, and days of supply regularly to assess inventory health and performance.
- Analyze root causes of inventory issues and identify opportunities for improvement using data analytics and performance dashboards.
- Continuously optimize inventory levels, reorder points, and replenishment strategies based on changing market conditions, demand patterns, and supply chain dynamics.

8. Risk Management and Contingency Planning:
- Identify and mitigate inventory-related risks such as stockouts, overstocking, obsolescence, and supply disruptions through risk assessment and contingency planning.
- Implement risk management strategies such as diversification, safety stock allocation, alternative sourcing, and supply chain resilience initiatives to minimize the impact of unforeseen events on inventory performance.

By implementing these inventory management strategies systematically and leveraging technology and data-driven approaches, companies can optimize inventory levels, improve supply chain efficiency, and enhance customer satisfaction while minimizing costs and risks.

AUGMENTED REALITY FOR ASSEMBLY AND MAINTENANCE

Augmented reality (AR) offers significant potential for enhancing assembly and maintenance tasks by providing workers with real-time digital information and guidance overlaid onto their physical environment. Here's how augmented reality can facilitate human-machine collaboration in assembly and maintenance processes:

1. Assembly Guidance:
   - AR can provide step-by-step instructions and visual aids overlaid onto physical objects, guiding workers through complex assembly processes.
   - Workers can see digital annotations, arrows, and animations overlaid onto parts, indicating assembly sequences, orientation, and connections.

2. Interactive Training:
   - AR can be used for interactive training sessions where workers can practice assembly procedures in a simulated environment overlaid with digital instructions and feedback.
   - Workers can learn assembly techniques and procedures in a hands-on, immersive manner, improving learning retention and reducing training time.

3. Remote Assistance:
   - AR enables remote experts to provide real-time guidance and

support to on-site workers during assembly and maintenance tasks.

- Workers can wear AR glasses or use handheld devices to stream live video of their workspace to remote experts, who can then overlay annotations and instructions onto the video feed, guiding the worker through the task.

4. Maintenance Support:

- AR can assist maintenance technicians by overlaying maintenance procedures, schematics, and diagnostic information onto equipment and machinery.

- Technicians can access equipment manuals, service history, and troubleshooting guides in real-time, reducing downtime and improving maintenance efficiency.

5. Digital Twin Integration:

- AR can integrate with digital twin models of equipment and machinery, providing workers with virtual representations overlaid onto physical assets.

- Workers can visualize equipment internals, identify components, and access real-time sensor data and performance metrics overlaid onto the digital twin representation.

6. Quality Assurance:

- AR can support quality assurance processes by overlaying inspection criteria, tolerance limits, and quality checkpoints onto physical parts and assemblies.

- Workers can perform visual inspections and measurements using AR tools, ensuring that parts meet quality standards before proceeding with assembly or installation.

7. Collaborative Workflows:

- AR facilitates collaborative workflows by enabling multiple workers to view and interact with the same digital information overlaid onto their shared physical environment.

- Workers can collaborate on assembly tasks, share annotations and notes, and coordinate activities in real-time using AR-enabled communication tools.

8. Data Capture and Documentation:

- AR can capture data and annotations created during assembly and maintenance tasks, providing a digital record of work performed.

- Workers can capture photos, videos, and annotations overlaid onto physical objects, creating documentation for future reference, training, and quality assurance purposes.

By leveraging augmented reality for assembly and maintenance tasks, companies can improve worker productivity, reduce errors, enhance training effectiveness, and streamline collaboration between humans and machines. AR-enabled workflows empower workers with digital tools and information, enabling them to perform tasks more efficiently and effectively in complex manufacturing and maintenance environments.

WORKER TRAINING USING VIRTUAL REALITY

Worker training using virtual reality (VR) offers immersive and interactive experiences that simulate real-world scenarios, providing a safe and effective environment for learning and skill development. Here's how virtual reality can facilitate worker training and collaboration:

1. Immersive Simulations:
   - VR enables workers to immerse themselves in realistic simulations of work environments, equipment, and processes.
   - Trainees can practice tasks and procedures in a controlled virtual environment without the risk of injury or damage to equipment.

2. Hands-on Practice:
   - VR provides a hands-on learning experience where trainees can interact with virtual objects, tools, and machinery as they would in the real world.
   - Trainees can manipulate virtual components, perform assembly tasks, and practice maintenance procedures, gaining practical skills and confidence in their abilities.

3. Interactive Feedback:
   - VR systems can provide interactive feedback and guidance to trainees in real-time as they perform tasks.
   - Trainees receive feedback on their actions, such as correct

tool usage, proper assembly techniques, and adherence to safety procedures, helping them learn and improve their skills.

4. Scenario-based Training:
- VR enables the creation of scenario-based training modules that simulate various work scenarios and challenges.
- Trainees can experience different scenarios, such as equipment malfunctions, emergencies, or challenging working conditions, and learn how to respond effectively.

5. Remote Training:
- VR technology allows for remote training sessions where trainees can participate from anywhere with an internet connection.
- Remote trainees can join virtual training sessions, interact with instructors and peers, and collaborate on group exercises and simulations.

6. Customized Training Programs:
- VR training programs can be customized to meet specific training objectives, job roles, and skill levels.
- Training modules can be tailored to address the unique requirements of different industries, equipment types, and job functions, ensuring relevance and effectiveness.

7. Performance Assessment:
- VR systems can track trainee performance and behavior during training sessions, capturing data on task completion times, accuracy, and adherence to procedures.
- Instructors can review performance metrics and provide personalized feedback and coaching to trainees, helping them identify areas for improvement.

8. Cost and Time Savings:
- VR training reduces the need for physical training facilities, equipment, and materials, resulting in cost savings for organizations.
- Trainees can complete training modules more efficiently in

VR, reducing training time and allowing them to gain skills faster.

By leveraging virtual reality for worker training, companies can improve learning outcomes, enhance safety, and accelerate skill development across a wide range of industries and job roles. VR-enabled training programs provide a cost-effective and scalable solution for organizations looking to invest in workforce development and human-machine collaboration.

ETHICAL CONSIDERATIONS AND CHALLENGES IN HUMAN-MACHINE COLLABORATION

Human-machine collaboration introduces various ethical considerations and challenges that organizations and societies need to address. Here are some of the key issues:

1. Job Displacement and Reskilling:
   - Challenge: Automation and AI technologies may lead to job displacement for workers whose tasks are automated. There is a need to reskill and retrain workers for new roles and tasks.
   - Ethical Consideration: Ensuring that workers are supported through reskilling programs and provided with opportunities for lifelong learning to adapt to changing job requirements.

2. Worker Safety and Well-being:
   - Challenge: Human-machine collaboration may introduce new safety risks and hazards, such as accidents involving robots or ergonomic issues with wearable technologies.
   - Ethical Consideration: Prioritizing worker safety and well-being by implementing safety protocols, ergonomic designs, and risk assessments for human-machine collaborative systems.

3. Privacy and Data Security:
   - Challenge: Human-machine collaboration often involves collecting and processing large amounts of data, raising concerns about privacy, data ownership, and data security.
   - Ethical Consideration: Protecting individuals' privacy rights, ensuring transparency in data collection and usage, and implementing robust data security measures to safeguard sensitive information.

4. Algorithmic Bias and Fairness:
   - Challenge: AI algorithms used in human-machine collaboration systems may exhibit biases based on race, gender, or other protected characteristics, leading to unfair outcomes or discrimination.
   - Ethical Consideration: Mitigating algorithmic bias through algorithmic transparency, fairness assessments, and diverse representation in algorithm development teams to ensure equitable outcomes for all individuals.

5. Autonomy and Control:
   - Challenge: Increasing autonomy of machines and AI systems raises questions about accountability, responsibility, and human oversight.
   - Ethical Consideration: Maintaining human control and oversight over AI systems, establishing clear guidelines for decision-making and intervention, and defining accountability frameworks to address errors or failures in automated systems.

6. Ethical Decision-Making by Machines:
   - Challenge: AI systems may face ethical dilemmas where they must make decisions with moral implications, such as autonomous vehicles deciding between different courses of action in a potential accident scenario.
   - Ethical Consideration: Developing ethical AI frameworks and decision-making algorithms that prioritize human safety, well-being, and societal values, and ensuring transparency and

accountability in AI decision-making processes.

7. Societal Impact and Inequality:
- Challenge: Human-machine collaboration may exacerbate societal inequalities, such as widening the digital divide or concentrating wealth and power in the hands of a few.
- Ethical Consideration: Addressing societal impacts of technology through policies and regulations that promote inclusivity, accessibility, and equitable distribution of benefits, and fostering public dialogue and engagement on ethical issues related to human-machine collaboration.

8. Long-Term Implications and Unintended Consequences:
- Challenge: Human-machine collaboration may have long-term implications and unintended consequences that are difficult to predict, such as shifts in employment patterns, changes in social dynamics, or unforeseen risks to human well-being.
- Ethical Consideration: Conducting ethical impact assessments and scenario planning to anticipate and mitigate potential risks and consequences of human-machine collaboration, and fostering a culture of ethical reflection and responsibility among technology developers and stakeholders.

Addressing these ethical considerations and challenges requires a multidisciplinary approach involving policymakers, technologists, ethicists, educators, and other stakeholders to ensure that human-machine collaboration advances societal values, fosters human flourishing, and promotes the common good.

INDUSTRY EXAMPLES OF SUCCESSFUL IMPLEMENTATIONS OF AI IN TV MANUFACTURING

Several successful implementations of AI in TV manufacturing have demonstrated significant improvements in efficiency, quality, and innovation. Here are a few industry examples:

1. Samsung Electronics:
   - Samsung has implemented AI technologies across its TV manufacturing processes to enhance efficiency and quality. For example, Samsung utilizes machine learning algorithms for predictive maintenance of manufacturing equipment, reducing downtime and maintenance costs.
   - Samsung's AI-based image processing technology, called Quantum AI, optimizes picture quality by analyzing and enhancing video content in real-time. This technology enhances the viewing experience for consumers by delivering sharper images, improved contrast, and more accurate colors.

2. LG Electronics:
   - LG has integrated AI-powered robotics and automation into its TV manufacturing facilities to streamline production and increase output. LG's AI-driven robots perform tasks such

as component assembly, quality inspection, and packaging, improving production efficiency and reducing errors.

- LG's ThinQ AI platform, featured in its smart TVs, utilizes machine learning algorithms to analyze user preferences and viewing habits, providing personalized content recommendations and voice control capabilities. This AI-driven user interface enhances the user experience and increases customer satisfaction.

3. Sony Corporation:

- Sony has implemented AI technologies in its TV manufacturing processes to optimize supply chain management and logistics. Sony uses predictive analytics and machine learning algorithms to forecast demand, optimize inventory levels, and improve delivery schedules, reducing costs and lead times.

- Sony's BRAVIA XR series of smart TVs incorporate Cognitive Processor XR, an AI-powered image processor that analyzes and replicates human perception for enhanced picture and sound quality. This AI-driven technology delivers immersive viewing experiences with realistic colors, contrast, and audio.

4. TCL Corporation:

- TCL has adopted AI-driven quality control systems in its TV manufacturing facilities to ensure product reliability and consistency. TCL's AI-based inspection systems use computer vision and machine learning algorithms to detect defects and anomalies in TV panels and components, minimizing manufacturing defects and reducing waste.

- TCL's AiPQ Engine, featured in its smart TVs, leverages AI algorithms to optimize picture quality in real-time. The AiPQ Engine analyzes content characteristics and ambient lighting conditions to adjust brightness, contrast, and color settings dynamically, delivering vivid and lifelike images to viewers.

5. Hisense Group:

- Hisense has implemented AI technologies in its TV

manufacturing processes to enhance product innovation and differentiation. Hisense's AI-driven design and development tools enable rapid prototyping and iteration of new TV models, accelerating time-to-market and fostering product innovation.

- Hisense's ULED XD technology, powered by AI algorithms, enhances picture quality by analyzing and optimizing backlight control for improved contrast and brightness. This AI-driven technology delivers a more immersive viewing experience with deeper blacks and brighter highlights.

6. Panasonic Corporation:

- Panasonic has integrated AI-driven predictive maintenance systems into its TV manufacturing facilities to improve equipment reliability and uptime. Panasonic's predictive maintenance algorithms analyze sensor data and equipment performance metrics to identify potential failures before they occur, enabling proactive maintenance and reducing unplanned downtime.

- Panasonic's My Home Screen smart TV platform utilizes AI-based content recommendations and voice control features to enhance the user experience. By analyzing user preferences and viewing habits, My Home Screen delivers personalized content suggestions and intuitive navigation options, increasing user engagement and satisfaction.

7. Vizio Inc.:

- Vizio has adopted AI technologies in its TV manufacturing processes to optimize energy efficiency and sustainability. Vizio's AI-driven power management systems analyze usage patterns and environmental factors to optimize power consumption and reduce energy waste, contributing to lower operating costs and environmental impact.

- Vizio's SmartCast operating system leverages AI algorithms for content discovery and streaming optimization. SmartCast uses machine learning to recommend personalized content based on user preferences and viewing history, enhancing the content consumption experience for users.

8. Skyworth Group:

- Skyworth has implemented AI-driven quality control and inspection systems in its TV manufacturing facilities to ensure product quality and reliability. Skyworth's AI-based defect detection algorithms analyze images and video footage of TV panels and components to identify manufacturing defects and abnormalities, ensuring consistent product quality.

- Skyworth's AI-enabled smart TVs feature voice control and natural language processing capabilities for hands-free operation. By integrating AI technologies into its smart TV ecosystem, Skyworth enhances user convenience and accessibility, making the viewing experience more intuitive and enjoyable.

9. Sharp Corporation:

- Sharp has implemented AI-driven supply chain optimization solutions to streamline its TV manufacturing processes. By leveraging AI algorithms for demand forecasting, inventory management, and logistics optimization, Sharp improves production efficiency, reduces costs, and enhances customer satisfaction.

- Sharp's Aquos line of smart TVs features AI-enhanced image processing technology for upscaling lower-resolution content to higher quality. The AI algorithms analyze and enhance image details in real-time, delivering sharper and more vibrant visuals to viewers.

10. Toshiba Corporation:

- Toshiba has integrated AI-driven predictive maintenance systems into its TV manufacturing facilities to improve equipment reliability and reduce maintenance costs. Toshiba's predictive maintenance algorithms analyze sensor data and historical maintenance records to predict equipment failures and schedule proactive maintenance, minimizing downtime and optimizing production uptime.

- Toshiba's REGZA line of smart TVs incorporates AI-powered audio enhancements for immersive sound experiences. The AI algorithms analyze audio content in real-time to optimize sound quality and spatial effects, delivering an enhanced audiovisual experience to viewers.

11. Philips (TP Vision):

- Philips has adopted AI-driven quality control solutions to ensure product consistency and reliability in its TV manufacturing processes. Philips' AI-based inspection systems use computer vision and machine learning algorithms to detect defects and anomalies in TV panels and components, reducing manufacturing defects and enhancing product quality.

- Philips' Ambilight technology, powered by AI algorithms, enhances the viewing experience by extending the on-screen content onto the surrounding walls. The AI-driven Ambilight system analyzes the color and brightness of on-screen content to synchronize ambient lighting effects, creating a more immersive and engaging viewing environment.

12. Haier Group:

- Haier has implemented AI-powered predictive analytics solutions to optimize its TV manufacturing operations and supply chain management processes. Haier's AI algorithms analyze production data, demand forecasts, and supply chain dynamics to optimize inventory levels, production schedules, and logistics operations, improving efficiency and reducing costs.

- Haier's Smart TV lineup features AI-enabled voice assistants and content recommendation systems for personalized user experiences. By integrating AI technologies into its smart TV ecosystem, Haier enhances user engagement, convenience, and satisfaction.

13. Xiaomi Corporation:

- Xiaomi utilizes AI technologies in TV manufacturing to optimize production processes and enhance product features. The company employs machine learning algorithms for demand forecasting and inventory management, ensuring efficient production planning and inventory optimization.

- Xiaomi's Mi TV series incorporates AI-powered image processing and audio enhancement technologies to deliver immersive viewing experiences. AI algorithms analyze content in real-time to enhance picture quality, optimize sound output, and provide personalized recommendations to users.

14. Konka Group:

- Konka has integrated AI-driven robotics and automation solutions into its TV manufacturing facilities to improve production efficiency and quality. AI-powered robots perform tasks such as component assembly, quality inspection, and packaging, reducing production cycle times and minimizing errors.

- Konka's smart TVs feature AI-enhanced content discovery and voice control capabilities for intuitive user experiences. AI algorithms analyze user preferences and viewing habits to recommend personalized content and enable hands-free operation through voice commands.

15. Sceptre Incorporated:

- Sceptre has implemented AI-based quality control systems to ensure product consistency and reliability in its TV manufacturing processes. AI-driven inspection technologies analyze visual and performance metrics to detect defects and anomalies, ensuring high-quality products for consumers.

- Sceptre's smart TVs leverage AI algorithms for voice recognition and natural language processing, enabling seamless integration with virtual assistants and smart home devices. Users can control their TVs and access content using voice commands, enhancing convenience and accessibility.

16. Element Electronics:

- Element Electronics utilizes AI-powered analytics for supply chain optimization and demand forecasting in TV manufacturing. By analyzing market trends, consumer preferences, and production data, Element Electronics optimizes inventory levels, production schedules, and distribution channels to meet customer demand efficiently.

- Element Electronics' smart TVs feature AI-driven content recommendation systems and voice-controlled user interfaces. AI algorithms analyze user behavior and content preferences to deliver personalized recommendations and streamline user interactions with the TV.

17. Roku, Inc.:
- Roku incorporates AI technologies into its smart TV platform to personalize the user experience and optimize content recommendations. Roku's AI algorithms analyze viewing habits, content preferences, and user interactions to curate personalized content feeds and recommendations for each user.

- Roku's smart TVs also utilize AI-powered voice search and natural language processing for hands-free navigation and content discovery. Users can use voice commands to search for content, control playback, and access various features and settings on their TVs.

18. Toshiba Visual Solutions Corporation:
- Toshiba Visual Solutions leverages AI-driven image processing technologies in its TV manufacturing processes to enhance picture quality and performance. The company's AI-powered image processors analyze and optimize color accuracy, contrast, and sharpness in real-time, delivering superior visual experiences to viewers.

- Toshiba's smart TVs feature AI-enhanced upscaling and noise reduction algorithms for improving the clarity and sharpness of lower-resolution content. The AI algorithms analyze image characteristics and apply advanced processing techniques to enhance image quality and detail.

19. Insignia Electronics:

- Insignia Electronics integrates AI-driven voice recognition and natural language processing capabilities into its smart TVs for intuitive user interaction. The company's AI-powered voice assistants enable users to control their TVs, search for content, and access various features using voice commands.

- Insignia's smart TVs also leverage AI algorithms for content recommendations and personalized user experiences. By analyzing user preferences and viewing habits, the TVs deliver tailored content suggestions and recommendations to enhance user engagement and satisfaction.

20. TCL Electronics Holdings Limited:

- TCL Electronics employs AI technologies in its TV manufacturing processes to optimize production efficiency and product quality. The company utilizes machine learning algorithms for predictive maintenance, supply chain optimization, and demand forecasting, improving operational performance and customer satisfaction.

- TCL's smart TVs feature AI-enhanced image processing and audio optimization technologies for immersive entertainment experiences. AI algorithms analyze content characteristics, ambient lighting conditions, and user preferences to deliver superior picture quality, sound performance, and user interactions.

21. Grundig:

- Grundig integrates AI-driven technologies into its TV manufacturing processes to enhance product performance and user experience. The company utilizes AI algorithms for image processing and optimization, delivering superior picture quality with enhanced color accuracy, contrast, and clarity.

- Grundig's smart TVs feature AI-powered content recommendation systems and voice control capabilities for intuitive user interaction. AI algorithms analyze user preferences, viewing habits, and content metadata to provide personalized recommendations and streamline user navigation.

22. Hisense Group:
- Hisense Group incorporates AI technologies into its TV manufacturing processes to optimize production efficiency and product quality. The company utilizes machine learning algorithms for predictive maintenance, quality control, and supply chain management, improving operational performance and reducing costs.
- Hisense's smart TVs leverage AI-driven image processing and audio enhancement technologies for immersive entertainment experiences. AI algorithms analyze content characteristics, optimize picture settings, and enhance sound quality to deliver an enhanced viewing and listening experience to users.

23. Bang & Olufsen:
- Bang & Olufsen integrates AI-driven technologies into its high-end TV manufacturing processes to deliver premium audiovisual experiences. The company utilizes AI algorithms for image enhancement, noise reduction, and color calibration, ensuring exceptional picture quality and color accuracy.
- Bang & Olufsen's smart TVs feature AI-powered sound optimization and room calibration capabilities for immersive audio experiences. AI algorithms analyze room acoustics, speaker configurations, and audio content to optimize sound reproduction and deliver lifelike audio performances.

24. Sharp Corporation:
- Sharp Corporation employs AI technologies in its TV manufacturing processes to enhance product innovation and user interaction. The company utilizes AI-driven design tools and simulation technologies to accelerate product development cycles and improve design efficiency.
- Sharp's smart TVs feature AI-powered voice assistants and content recommendation systems for personalized user

experiences. AI algorithms analyze user preferences, voice commands, and content metadata to deliver tailored content suggestions and hands-free control options.

25. Metz Consumer Electronics GmbH:

- Metz Consumer Electronics integrates AI-driven technologies into its TV manufacturing processes to deliver high-quality products and services. The company utilizes AI algorithms for image processing, noise reduction, and motion enhancement, ensuring superior picture quality and motion clarity.

- Metz's smart TVs feature AI-powered content discovery and recommendation systems for personalized user experiences. AI algorithms analyze user preferences, viewing habits, and content metadata to provide tailored recommendations and enhance user engagement.

These industry examples demonstrate how AI technologies are transforming TV manufacturing by improving efficiency, quality, and innovation across various stages of the production process. By leveraging AI-driven solutions, TV manufacturers can enhance competitiveness, meet customer expectations, and drive growth in the rapidly evolving consumer electronics market.

BEST PRACTICES

Implementing AI in TV manufacturing involves several best practices to ensure successful outcomes. Here are some key considerations:

1. Clear Objectives: Define clear objectives and goals for implementing AI in TV manufacturing. Determine the specific problems or challenges AI will address, such as improving efficiency, quality, or innovation.

2. Cross-functional Collaboration: Foster collaboration between different departments and teams involved in TV manufacturing, including engineering, production, IT, and data science. Ensure alignment on objectives, requirements, and priorities across the organization.

3. Data Quality and Accessibility: Ensure access to high-quality data for AI model training and analysis. Collect and curate relevant data from various sources, including production systems, sensors, and quality control processes. Maintain data integrity, accuracy, and security throughout the data lifecycle.

4. Pilot Projects and Proof of Concepts: Start with pilot projects or proof of concepts to validate AI technologies and assess their feasibility and impact in TV manufacturing. Test different AI algorithms, tools, and methodologies in controlled environments before scaling up implementation.

5. Scalable Infrastructure: Invest in scalable IT infrastructure and computing resources to support AI model development, training, and deployment. Leverage cloud computing services

or high-performance computing platforms to handle large-scale data processing and AI workloads efficiently.

6. Talent Development: Invest in talent development and training programs to build AI capabilities within the organization. Recruit or upskill employees with expertise in data science, machine learning, and AI technologies to support AI initiatives effectively.

7. Ethical Considerations: Consider ethical implications and societal impacts of AI technologies in TV manufacturing. Ensure transparency, fairness, and accountability in AI-driven decision-making processes. Address concerns related to data privacy, bias, and algorithmic transparency.

8. Continuous Monitoring and Improvement: Implement mechanisms for continuous monitoring and evaluation of AI systems in TV manufacturing. Monitor performance metrics, user feedback, and business outcomes to assess the effectiveness of AI solutions and identify areas for improvement.

9. Regulatory Compliance: Ensure compliance with relevant regulations and industry standards governing AI technologies in TV manufacturing. Stay informed about emerging regulations related to data privacy, cybersecurity, and product safety, and adjust AI strategies accordingly.

10. User-Centric Design: Design AI-driven solutions with a focus on user experience and usability. Consider the needs and preferences of end-users, such as production workers, quality inspectors, and consumers, when designing AI-enabled products, processes, and interfaces.

11. Iterative Approach: Adopt an iterative approach to AI implementation in TV manufacturing. Continuously iterate and refine AI models, algorithms, and workflows based on feedback, data insights, and changing business requirements.

12. Partnerships and Ecosystem Collaboration: Explore

partnerships and collaboration opportunities with technology vendors, research institutions, and industry peers to leverage expertise, share best practices, and accelerate AI adoption in TV manufacturing.

By following these best practices, TV manufacturers can effectively harness the power of AI to drive innovation, improve operational efficiency, and deliver superior products and services to customers.

LESSONS LEARNED

Implementing AI in TV manufacturing comes with its own set of challenges and opportunities. Here are some key lessons learned from previous implementations:

1. Start Small, Scale Gradually: Begin with pilot projects or proof of concepts to test AI technologies in controlled environments. Start with specific use cases or processes where AI can deliver measurable benefits, and then scale up gradually based on successful outcomes.

2. Data Quality is Crucial: High-quality data is essential for training accurate AI models. Invest in data collection, preprocessing, and validation processes to ensure data quality and reliability. Clean, relevant, and well-labeled data is essential for building effective AI solutions.

3. Domain Expertise is Essential: Domain expertise is critical for understanding the intricacies of TV manufacturing processes and identifying opportunities for AI-driven improvements. Collaborate closely with domain experts, production engineers, and frontline workers to develop AI solutions that address real-world challenges effectively.

4. Interdisciplinary Collaboration: Successful AI implementations in TV manufacturing require interdisciplinary collaboration between data scientists, engineers, production managers, and other stakeholders. Foster collaboration and communication across different departments and teams to ensure alignment on objectives, requirements, and priorities.

5. Continuous Learning and Adaptation: AI technologies evolve rapidly, and continuous learning and adaptation are essential for staying ahead. Invest in talent development, training programs, and knowledge sharing initiatives to keep pace with advancements in AI and machine learning.

6. Ethical Considerations: Consider ethical implications and societal impacts of AI technologies in TV manufacturing. Ensure transparency, fairness, and accountability in AI-driven decision-making processes. Address concerns related to data privacy, bias, and algorithmic transparency to build trust among stakeholders.

7. User Feedback Drives Improvement: Solicit feedback from end-users, including production workers, quality inspectors, and consumers, to understand their needs and preferences. Incorporate user feedback into the design and refinement of AI-driven solutions to ensure they meet user expectations and deliver value.

8. Regulatory Compliance: Stay informed about regulations and industry standards governing AI technologies in TV manufacturing. Ensure compliance with data privacy regulations, product safety standards, and other relevant requirements to mitigate risks and maintain trust with customers and regulators.

9. Focus on Business Outcomes: Align AI initiatives with business objectives and focus on delivering tangible business outcomes, such as improved efficiency, quality, and innovation. Measure the impact of AI implementations using key performance indicators (KPIs) and adjust strategies accordingly to maximize ROI.

10. Long-Term Vision and Strategy: Develop a long-term vision and strategy for AI adoption in TV manufacturing. Consider how AI technologies can drive innovation, competitive

advantage, and sustainable growth in the rapidly evolving consumer electronics market.

By applying these lessons learned, TV manufacturers can navigate the complexities of AI implementation effectively and unlock the full potential of AI to transform their operations and deliver value to customers.

FUTURE TRENDS AND EMERGING TECHNOLOGIES

The future of AI in TV manufacturing holds several exciting trends and emerging technologies that are likely to shape the industry. Here are some key trends to watch for:

1. Advanced Image Processing: Continued advancements in AI-driven image processing technologies will enhance picture quality and visual performance in TVs. Techniques such as neural network-based upscaling, noise reduction, and dynamic HDR optimization will deliver sharper, more vibrant images with higher levels of detail and realism.

2. Personalized Viewing Experiences: AI algorithms will enable personalized content recommendations, user interfaces, and viewing experiences tailored to individual preferences and viewing habits. Advanced user profiling, content analysis, and recommendation engines will deliver personalized content feeds, curated playlists, and intuitive navigation options for users.

3. Voice and Gesture Control: AI-powered voice recognition and gesture control will become increasingly prevalent in smart TVs, enabling hands-free operation and intuitive user interactions. Natural language processing algorithms will enable seamless voice commands for content navigation, search, and device

control.

4. Context-Aware Viewing: AI technologies will enable TVs to become more context-aware, adjusting settings and content recommendations based on factors such as time of day, user location, and ambient lighting conditions. Contextual analysis and sensor integration will enhance the viewing experience and optimize energy efficiency.

5. Integration with Smart Home Ecosystems: Smart TVs will integrate more seamlessly with smart home ecosystems, leveraging AI-driven interoperability and automation capabilities. Integration with voice assistants, home automation platforms, and IoT devices will enable unified control and synchronization of smart home devices and services.

6. Enhanced Audio Experiences: AI-driven audio processing technologies will enhance sound quality and spatial immersion in TVs. Techniques such as virtual surround sound, adaptive audio equalization, and room acoustics optimization will deliver more immersive and lifelike audio experiences to viewers.

7. Predictive Maintenance and Self-Healing Systems: AI-driven predictive maintenance systems will become standard in TV manufacturing, enabling proactive identification and resolution of equipment failures and performance degradation. Predictive analytics and machine learning algorithms will optimize maintenance schedules, reduce downtime, and extend the lifespan of TV components.

8. Augmented Reality Integration: Augmented reality (AR) technologies will enhance the installation, setup, and maintenance of TVs through interactive guides, remote assistance, and real-time visualization tools. AR-enabled user interfaces and applications will provide intuitive guidance and troubleshooting support for users and technicians.

9. Environmental Sustainability: AI technologies will play a significant role in improving environmental sustainability in TV manufacturing. Optimization algorithms, energy management systems, and eco-friendly materials will reduce energy consumption, minimize waste, and lower the carbon footprint of TV production processes.

10. AI-driven Content Creation and Enhancement: AI algorithms will be increasingly used to create and enhance TV content, including upscaling lower-resolution content, removing artifacts, and generating immersive visual effects. AI-driven content generation tools will enable filmmakers and content creators to unleash their creativity and deliver compelling viewing experiences.

Overall, the future of AI in TV manufacturing is bright, with continued advancements driving innovation, personalization, and sustainability in the industry. By embracing these trends and emerging technologies, TV manufacturers can stay competitive, meet evolving consumer demands, and deliver next-generation products and experiences to users.

ADDRESSING CHALLENGES IN AI ADOPTION

AI adoption in TV manufacturing faces several challenges that need to be addressed to realize its full potential. Here are some key challenges and strategies to overcome them:

1. Data Quality and Accessibility: Challenge: Lack of high-quality, labeled data for training AI models is a significant barrier to adoption. Data may be fragmented, incomplete, or inaccessible across different departments and systems.
   - Strategy: Invest in data collection, preprocessing, and validation processes to ensure data quality and accessibility. Establish data governance frameworks, data sharing protocols, and data integration solutions to centralize and standardize data across the organization.

2. Technical Complexity and Skills Gap: Challenge: Implementing AI technologies requires specialized technical expertise in data science, machine learning, and AI development, which may be lacking within the organization.
   - Strategy: Invest in talent development and training programs to build AI capabilities within the organization. Recruit or upskill employees with expertise in data science, machine learning, and AI technologies. Leverage external partnerships, consulting services, or training courses to supplement internal expertise.

3. Integration with Existing Systems: Challenge: Integrating AI solutions with existing IT infrastructure, legacy systems, and production processes can be complex and time-consuming. Compatibility issues, data silos, and interoperability challenges may hinder seamless integration.

- Strategy: Develop a comprehensive integration strategy that aligns AI initiatives with existing systems and processes. Prioritize interoperability, scalability, and flexibility when selecting AI platforms and technologies. Collaborate with IT and operations teams to ensure smooth integration and minimize disruptions.

4. Ethical and Regulatory Considerations: Challenge: AI adoption raises ethical concerns related to data privacy, bias, transparency, and accountability. Regulatory compliance with data protection laws, industry standards, and ethical guidelines is essential but challenging to navigate.

- Strategy: Establish clear ethical guidelines and governance frameworks for AI adoption, covering data privacy, algorithmic bias, transparency, and accountability. Conduct ethical impact assessments and risk analyses to identify and mitigate potential ethical issues. Stay informed about evolving regulations and standards governing AI technologies in TV manufacturing.

5. Cost and Return on Investment (ROI): Challenge: Implementing AI technologies involves significant upfront costs, including investment in hardware, software, talent, and infrastructure. Demonstrating measurable ROI and business value can be challenging, especially in the short term.

- Strategy: Develop a comprehensive business case and ROI analysis to justify AI investments and secure buy-in from stakeholders. Focus on quantifiable metrics such as cost savings, productivity gains, quality improvements, and revenue growth. Start with low-cost, high-impact pilot projects to demonstrate proof of concept and build momentum for broader adoption.

6. Change Management and Cultural Shift: Challenge: Adopting AI requires a cultural shift within the organization, including changes in mindset, processes, and workflows. Resistance to change, fear of job displacement, and lack of buy-in from employees and leadership can impede adoption.

- Strategy: Foster a culture of innovation, collaboration, and continuous learning to support AI adoption efforts. Communicate the benefits of AI adoption transparently and engage employees at all levels in the process. Provide training, support, and incentives to empower employees to embrace AI technologies and adapt to new ways of working.

7. Security and Privacy Concerns: Challenge: AI adoption introduces security and privacy risks, including data breaches, unauthorized access, and misuse of sensitive information. Protecting data privacy and ensuring cybersecurity resilience is essential but challenging in the face of evolving threats.

- Strategy: Implement robust cybersecurity measures, encryption protocols, access controls, and data anonymization techniques to protect sensitive data and AI models. Conduct regular security audits, vulnerability assessments, and penetration testing to identify and mitigate security risks. Comply with data protection regulations and industry standards to safeguard customer privacy and trust.

Addressing these challenges requires a holistic approach that encompasses technical, organizational, ethical, and regulatory considerations. By proactively identifying and mitigating these challenges, TV manufacturers can accelerate AI adoption, unlock value, and drive innovation in the industry.

REGULATORY AND ETHICAL CONSIDERATIONS

In the context of AI adoption in TV manufacturing, regulatory and ethical considerations play a crucial role in ensuring responsible use of AI technologies and protecting the interests of stakeholders. Here are some key regulatory and ethical considerations:

1. Data Privacy: TV manufacturers must comply with data privacy regulations, such as the General Data Protection Regulation (GDPR) in the European Union and the California Consumer Privacy Act (CCPA) in the United States. These regulations govern the collection, storage, processing, and sharing of personal data and require companies to obtain explicit consent from individuals before collecting or using their data.

2. Algorithmic Bias and Fairness: TV manufacturers must address concerns related to algorithmic bias, which can lead to unfair outcomes or discrimination. AI algorithms may inadvertently perpetuate biases present in training data, leading to biased decision-making processes. It's essential to implement measures to detect, mitigate, and prevent algorithmic bias, such as algorithmic transparency, fairness assessments, and diverse representation in data and algorithm development.

3. Transparency and Explainability: AI algorithms used in TV manufacturing should be transparent and explainable, enabling users to understand how decisions are made and the factors influencing those decisions. Transparency and explainability promote trust, accountability, and ethical use of AI technologies, particularly in safety-critical applications such as autonomous systems and predictive maintenance.

4. Consumer Protection: TV manufacturers have a responsibility to ensure the safety, reliability, and quality of their products and services. AI-driven features and functionalities should undergo rigorous testing, validation, and certification processes to meet industry standards and regulatory requirements. Manufacturers should provide clear and accurate information to consumers about AI-enabled features, potential risks, and limitations.

5. Product Liability and Accountability: TV manufacturers may be held liable for damages caused by AI-driven products or services, particularly in cases of malfunction, failure, or misuse. Manufacturers should establish accountability frameworks, risk management processes, and liability policies to address potential legal and ethical implications of AI adoption. They should also provide adequate training and support to users to minimize the risk of misuse or unintended consequences.

6. Intellectual Property Rights: TV manufacturers should respect intellectual property rights and ensure compliance with patent, copyright, and trademark laws when developing and deploying AI technologies. Manufacturers should obtain necessary licenses or permissions for using third-party algorithms, datasets, or proprietary technologies and adhere to best practices for intellectual property protection and licensing agreements.

7. Environmental Impact: TV manufacturers should consider the environmental impact of AI adoption, including

energy consumption, resource usage, and electronic waste generation. Manufacturers should strive to develop energy-efficient products, optimize production processes, and promote sustainable practices throughout the product lifecycle, from design and manufacturing to end-of-life disposal and recycling.

8. International Standards and Guidelines: TV manufacturers should adhere to international standards, guidelines, and best practices for AI development and deployment, such as the IEEE Ethically Aligned Design principles, the ISO/IEC 27701 standard for privacy information management, and the OECD Principles on Artificial Intelligence. Compliance with these standards helps ensure ethical and responsible use of AI technologies on a global scale.

By addressing these regulatory and ethical considerations, TV manufacturers can promote responsible AI adoption, build trust with consumers and stakeholders, and contribute to the ethical advancement of AI technologies in the TV manufacturing industry.

FUTURE PROSPECTS OF AI IN TV MANUFACTURING

The future prospects of AI in TV manufacturing are promising, with continued advancements in AI technologies poised to revolutionize the industry. Here are some key future prospects:

1. Enhanced Product Innovation: AI technologies will enable TV manufacturers to innovate and differentiate their products by delivering new features, functionalities, and user experiences. AI-driven image processing, audio enhancement, and content recommendation systems will enable TVs to deliver superior picture quality, immersive sound, and personalized viewing experiences.

2. Optimized Production Processes: AI will optimize production processes in TV manufacturing, leading to increased efficiency, quality, and cost-effectiveness. AI-driven predictive maintenance, supply chain optimization, and production scheduling will minimize downtime, reduce waste, and streamline operations, resulting in higher productivity and profitability.

3. Personalized User Experiences: AI will enable TV manufacturers to deliver personalized user experiences tailored to individual preferences and viewing habits. AI-driven content recommendation systems, voice assistants, and user interfaces

will provide personalized content suggestions, intuitive navigation options, and seamless integration with smart home ecosystems, enhancing user satisfaction and engagement.

4. Integration with Smart Home Ecosystems: Smart TVs will integrate more seamlessly with smart home ecosystems, leveraging AI-driven interoperability and automation capabilities. Integration with voice assistants, home automation platforms, and IoT devices will enable unified control and synchronization of smart home devices and services, enhancing convenience and connectivity for users.

5. Predictive Maintenance and Self-Healing Systems: AI-driven predictive maintenance systems will become standard in TV manufacturing, enabling proactive identification and resolution of equipment failures and performance degradation. Predictive analytics and machine learning algorithms will optimize maintenance schedules, reduce downtime, and extend the lifespan of TV components, ensuring reliable and durable products for consumers.

6. Environmental Sustainability: AI technologies will play a significant role in improving environmental sustainability in TV manufacturing. Optimization algorithms, energy management systems, and eco-friendly materials will reduce energy consumption, minimize waste, and lower the carbon footprint of TV production processes, aligning with industry trends towards sustainability and green manufacturing practices.

7. Augmented Reality Integration: Augmented reality (AR) technologies will enhance the installation, setup, and maintenance of TVs through interactive guides, remote assistance, and real-time visualization tools. AR-enabled user interfaces and applications will provide intuitive guidance and troubleshooting support for users and technicians, improving user experience and service efficiency.

8. AI-driven Content Creation and Enhancement: AI algorithms

will be increasingly used to create and enhance TV content, including upscaling lower-resolution content, removing artifacts, and generating immersive visual effects. AI-driven content generation tools will enable filmmakers and content creators to unleash their creativity and deliver compelling viewing experiences, driving innovation and differentiation in the industry.

Overall, AI will continue to drive innovation, efficiency, and personalization in TV manufacturing, shaping the future of the industry and delivering enhanced products and experiences to consumers. As AI technologies continue to evolve, TV manufacturers will leverage these capabilities to stay competitive, meet evolving consumer demands, and drive growth in the dynamic and rapidly evolving consumer electronics market.

CASE STUDY: IMPLEMENTING PREDICTIVE MAINTENANCE WITH AI IN TV MANUFACTURING

Introduction:
ABC Electronics, a leading TV manufacturer, is looking to improve the reliability and efficiency of its production processes. One of their key objectives is to minimize unplanned downtime and optimize maintenance schedules to ensure uninterrupted production. To achieve this goal, ABC Electronics decides to implement predictive maintenance using AI technologies.

Objective:
The objective of this project is to develop an AI-driven predictive maintenance system that can analyze sensor data from manufacturing equipment and predict potential equipment failures before they occur. By proactively identifying maintenance needs, ABC Electronics aims to reduce downtime, extend equipment lifespan, and optimize maintenance costs.

Approach:
ABC Electronics collects historical sensor data from manufacturing equipment, including temperature, vibration, and operational parameters. They leverage machine learning algorithms to analyze this data and develop predictive models capable of identifying patterns indicative of impending equipment failures.

Python Code:
Below is a simplified example of how ABC Electronics can implement predictive maintenance using Python and scikit-learn, a popular machine learning library:

```python
# Importing necessary libraries
import pandas as pd
from sklearn.model_selection import train_test_split
from sklearn.ensemble import RandomForestClassifier
from sklearn.metrics import accuracy_score

# Load sensor data
sensor_data = pd.read_csv('sensor_data.csv')

# Preprocess data
# Drop irrelevant columns
sensor_data.drop(['timestamp'], axis=1, inplace=True)

# Split data into features and target variable
X = sensor_data.drop('failure', axis=1)
y = sensor_data['failure']

# Split data into training and testing sets
X_train, X_test, y_train, y_test = train_test_split(X, y, test_size=0.2, random_state=42)

# Train Random Forest classifier
clf = RandomForestClassifier(n_estimators=100, random_state=42)
```

```
clf.fit(X_train, y_train)

# Predict on test data
y_pred = clf.predict(X_test)

# Evaluate model performance
accuracy = accuracy_score(y_test, y_pred)
print("Accuracy:", accuracy)
` ` `
```

Results:
After training the Random Forest classifier on historical sensor data, ABC Electronics achieves an accuracy of 95% in predicting equipment failures. The predictive maintenance system can now analyze real-time sensor data and alert maintenance teams of potential issues before they escalate into costly breakdowns.

Conclusion:
By implementing predictive maintenance with AI technologies, ABC Electronics has successfully improved the reliability and efficiency of its production processes. The AI-driven system enables proactive maintenance, reduces downtime, and optimizes maintenance costs, ultimately enhancing operational performance and competitiveness in the TV manufacturing industry.

CASE STUDY: IMPLEMENTING COMPUTER VISION FOR QUALITY INSPECTION IN TV MANUFACTURING

Introduction:
XYZ Electronics, a leading TV manufacturer, is committed to delivering high-quality products to its customers. However, manual inspection processes are time-consuming and prone to errors, leading to inefficiencies and quality issues. To address this challenge, XYZ Electronics decides to implement computer vision with AI technologies for automated quality inspection in its TV manufacturing facility.

Objective:
The objective of this project is to develop a computer vision system capable of automatically inspecting TV components for defects and anomalies during the manufacturing process. By leveraging AI algorithms and image processing techniques, XYZ Electronics aims to improve inspection accuracy, increase throughput, and ensure consistent product quality.

Approach:
XYZ Electronics collects images of TV components at various stages of the manufacturing process, including circuit boards, display panels, and casings. They annotate the images to label defects and non-defective components for training the computer vision model. Using deep learning algorithms, they train a convolutional neural network (CNN) to classify images and detect defects accurately.

Python Code:
Below is a simplified example of how XYZ Electronics can implement computer vision for quality inspection using Python and TensorFlow, a popular deep learning framework:

```python
# Importing necessary libraries
import tensorflow as tf
from tensorflow.keras.models import Sequential
from tensorflow.keras.layers import Conv2D, MaxPooling2D, Flatten, Dense
from tensorflow.keras.preprocessing.image import ImageDataGenerator

# Set random seed for reproducibility
tf.random.set_seed(42)

# Define CNN model architecture
model = Sequential([
    Conv2D(32, (3, 3), activation='relu', input_shape=(128, 128, 3)),
    MaxPooling2D((2, 2)),
    Conv2D(64, (3, 3), activation='relu'),
    MaxPooling2D((2, 2)),
    Conv2D(128, (3, 3), activation='relu'),
    MaxPooling2D((2, 2)),
    Flatten(),
    Dense(128, activation='relu'),
```

```
    Dense(1, activation='sigmoid')
])

# Compile model
model.compile(optimizer='adam',
        loss='binary_crossentropy',
        metrics=['accuracy'])

# Load and preprocess image data
train_datagen    =    ImageDataGenerator(rescale=1./255,
shear_range=0.2, zoom_range=0.2, horizontal_flip=True)
train_generator                                    =
train_datagen.flow_from_directory('train_data',
target_size=(128, 128), batch_size=32, class_mode='binary')

# Train model
history    =    model.fit(train_generator,    epochs=10,
steps_per_epoch=len(train_generator))

# Save model
model.save('quality_inspection_model.h5')
` ` `
```

Results:
After training the CNN model on annotated image data, XYZ Electronics achieves high accuracy in detecting defects during quality inspection. The computer vision system can now analyze images of TV components in real-time and identify defects such as cracks, scratches, and soldering errors with high precision and reliability.

Conclusion:
By implementing computer vision with AI technologies for quality inspection, XYZ Electronics has transformed its manufacturing processes, improving efficiency, and ensuring consistent product quality. The AI-driven system enables automated defect detection, reduces reliance on manual inspection, and enhances overall production efficiency in the TV

manufacturing industry.

CASE STUDY: IMPLEMENTING PREDICTIVE MAINTENANCE WITH AI IN TV MANUFACTURING

Introduction:
ABC Electronics, a prominent TV manufacturer, faces challenges with equipment breakdowns and unplanned downtime in its manufacturing facilities. To address these issues and improve operational efficiency, ABC Electronics decides to implement predictive maintenance using AI technologies.

Objective:
The objective of this project is to develop an AI-driven predictive maintenance system capable of analyzing sensor data from manufacturing equipment to predict potential failures before they occur. By identifying maintenance needs in advance, ABC Electronics aims to minimize downtime, reduce maintenance costs, and optimize production efficiency.

Approach:
ABC Electronics collects historical sensor data from

manufacturing equipment, including temperature, vibration, and operating parameters. They use machine learning algorithms to analyze this data and develop predictive models capable of identifying patterns indicative of impending equipment failures. The Python code below demonstrates how ABC Electronics can implement predictive maintenance using a Random Forest classifier:

Python Code:

```python
# Importing necessary libraries
import pandas as pd
from sklearn.model_selection import train_test_split
from sklearn.ensemble import RandomForestClassifier
from sklearn.metrics import accuracy_score

# Load sensor data
sensor_data = pd.read_csv('sensor_data.csv')

# Preprocess data
# Drop irrelevant columns
sensor_data.drop(['timestamp'], axis=1, inplace=True)

# Split data into features and target variable
X = sensor_data.drop('failure', axis=1)
y = sensor_data['failure']

# Split data into training and testing sets
X_train, X_test, y_train, y_test = train_test_split(X, y, test_size=0.2, random_state=42)

# Train Random Forest classifier
clf = RandomForestClassifier(n_estimators=100, random_state=42)
clf.fit(X_train, y_train)

# Predict on test data
y_pred = clf.predict(X_test)
```

```
# Evaluate model performance
accuracy = accuracy_score(y_test, y_pred)
print("Accuracy:", accuracy)
` ` `
```

Results:
After training the Random Forest classifier on historical sensor data, ABC Electronics achieves an accuracy of 95% in predicting equipment failures. The predictive maintenance system can now analyze real-time sensor data and alert maintenance teams of potential issues before they escalate into costly breakdowns.

Conclusion:
By implementing predictive maintenance with AI technologies, ABC Electronics has significantly improved the reliability and efficiency of its production processes. The AI-driven system enables proactive maintenance, reduces downtime, and optimizes maintenance costs, ultimately enhancing operational performance and competitiveness in the TV manufacturing industry.

CASE STUDY: AI-ENABLED DEFECT DETECTION IN TV MANUFACTURING

Introduction:
XYZ Electronics, a leading TV manufacturer, aims to enhance the quality control process in its manufacturing facilities. Traditional methods of visual inspection are time-consuming and prone to human error, leading to inefficiencies and increased production costs. To address these challenges, XYZ Electronics decides to implement AI-enabled defect detection using computer vision technology.

Objective:
The objective of this project is to develop a computer vision system capable of automatically detecting defects in TV components during the manufacturing process. By leveraging AI algorithms, XYZ Electronics aims to improve inspection accuracy, reduce false positives, and streamline the quality control process.

Approach:
XYZ Electronics collects a dataset of images of TV components, including circuit boards, display panels, and casings, both with and without defects. They annotate the images to label defects such as scratches, dents, and soldering errors. Using

deep learning techniques, XYZ Electronics trains a convolutional neural network (CNN) to classify images and identify defects accurately.

Python Code:
Below is a simplified example of how XYZ Electronics can implement AI-enabled defect detection using Python and TensorFlow, a popular deep learning framework:

```python
# Importing necessary libraries
import tensorflow as tf
from tensorflow.keras.models import Sequential
from tensorflow.keras.layers import Conv2D, MaxPooling2D, Flatten, Dense
from tensorflow.keras.preprocessing.image import ImageDataGenerator

# Set random seed for reproducibility
tf.random.set_seed(42)

# Define CNN model architecture
model = Sequential([
    Conv2D(32, (3, 3), activation='relu', input_shape=(128, 128, 3)),
    MaxPooling2D((2, 2)),
    Conv2D(64, (3, 3), activation='relu'),
    MaxPooling2D((2, 2)),
    Conv2D(128, (3, 3), activation='relu'),
    MaxPooling2D((2, 2)),
    Flatten(),
    Dense(128, activation='relu'),
    Dense(1, activation='sigmoid')
])

# Compile model
model.compile(optimizer='adam',
          loss='binary_crossentropy',
```

```
        metrics=['accuracy'])

# Load and preprocess image data
train_datagen      =        ImageDataGenerator(rescale=1./255,
shear_range=0.2, zoom_range=0.2, horizontal_flip=True)
train_generator                                            =
train_datagen.flow_from_directory('train_data',
target_size=(128, 128), batch_size=32, class_mode='binary')

# Train model
history      =        model.fit(train_generator,      epochs=10,
steps_per_epoch=len(train_generator))

# Save model
model.save('defect_detection_model.h5')
` ` `
```

Results:
After training the CNN model on annotated image data, XYZ
Electronics achieves high accuracy in detecting defects during
quality inspection. The computer vision system can now
analyze images of TV components in real-time and identify
defects such as cracks, scratches, and soldering errors with high
precision and reliability.

Conclusion:
By implementing AI-enabled defect detection with computer
vision technology, XYZ Electronics has revolutionized its quality
control process. The AI-driven system enables automated defect
detection, reduces reliance on manual inspection, and enhances
overall production efficiency in the TV manufacturing industry.

CASE STUDY: AI OPTIMIZATION OF TV MANUFACTURING PROCESSES

Introduction:
ABC Electronics, a leading TV manufacturer, is looking to leverage AI to enhance its manufacturing processes. With the increasing demand for TVs and the need to stay competitive in the market, ABC Electronics aims to improve efficiency, reduce costs, and enhance product quality through AI-driven optimization.

Objective:
The objective of this project is to implement AI technologies across various stages of TV manufacturing to streamline processes, increase productivity, and improve overall performance. This includes optimizing supply chain management, enhancing quality control, and implementing predictive maintenance.

Approach:
ABC Electronics adopts a phased approach to implement AI across its manufacturing processes:

1. Supply Chain Optimization: ABC Electronics implements AI-driven supply chain management to optimize inventory levels,

reduce lead times, and improve supplier relationships. They use machine learning algorithms to forecast demand, optimize procurement, and identify cost-saving opportunities.

2. Quality Control Enhancement: ABC Electronics deploys computer vision and machine learning algorithms for automated quality control. They develop AI models capable of detecting defects in TV components with high accuracy, reducing the need for manual inspection and ensuring consistent product quality.

3. Predictive Maintenance Implementation: ABC Electronics integrates AI-powered predictive maintenance systems into its manufacturing equipment. They collect sensor data from production machinery and use AI algorithms to predict equipment failures before they occur, minimizing downtime and optimizing maintenance schedules.

Python Code (Sample for Predictive Maintenance Implementation):
Below is a simplified example of how ABC Electronics can implement predictive maintenance using Python and scikit-learn, a popular machine learning library:

```python
# Importing necessary libraries
import pandas as pd
from sklearn.model_selection import train_test_split
from sklearn.ensemble import RandomForestClassifier
from sklearn.metrics import accuracy_score

# Load sensor data
sensor_data = pd.read_csv('sensor_data.csv')

# Preprocess data
# Drop irrelevant columns
sensor_data.drop(['timestamp'], axis=1, inplace=True)

# Split data into features and target variable
```

```
X = sensor_data.drop('failure', axis=1)
y = sensor_data['failure']

# Split data into training and testing sets
X_train, X_test, y_train, y_test = train_test_split(X, y,
test_size=0.2, random_state=42)

# Train Random Forest classifier
clf = RandomForestClassifier(n_estimators=100,
random_state=42)
clf.fit(X_train, y_train)

# Predict on test data
y_pred = clf.predict(X_test)

# Evaluate model performance
accuracy = accuracy_score(y_test, y_pred)
print("Accuracy:", accuracy)
```

Results:
By implementing AI optimization across its manufacturing processes, ABC Electronics achieves significant improvements in efficiency, cost reduction, and product quality. The AI-driven supply chain management system improves inventory management and reduces procurement costs, while automated quality control enhances product consistency and reliability. Predictive maintenance minimizes equipment downtime and ensures smooth production operations, ultimately enhancing ABC Electronics' competitiveness in the TV manufacturing industry.

Conclusion:
Through the strategic implementation of AI technologies, ABC Electronics transforms its TV manufacturing processes, driving efficiency, quality, and innovation. By leveraging AI for supply chain optimization, quality control enhancement, and predictive maintenance, ABC Electronics achieves operational

excellence and maintains its position as a leader in the competitive TV manufacturing market.

CASE STUDY: AI-DRIVEN QUALITY CONTROL IN TV MANUFACTURING

Introduction:
XYZ Electronics is a leading manufacturer of high-definition televisions. To maintain its reputation for quality and reliability, XYZ Electronics is exploring ways to enhance its quality control processes using artificial intelligence (AI). The company aims to leverage AI technologies to automate defect detection and improve the efficiency and accuracy of its manufacturing operations.

Objective:
The objective of this project is to implement a computer vision-based quality control system that can automatically detect defects in TV components during the manufacturing process. By integrating AI into its quality control process, XYZ Electronics aims to reduce human error, increase throughput, and ensure consistent product quality.

Approach:
XYZ Electronics adopts the following approach to implement AI-driven quality control in its TV manufacturing process:

1. Data Collection: XYZ Electronics collects a large dataset of

images of TV components, including circuit boards, display panels, and casings, both with and without defects. These images serve as the training data for the AI model.

2. Data Annotation: XYZ Electronics annotates the images to label defects such as scratches, dents, and soldering errors. This step is crucial for training the AI model to accurately identify and classify defects in the images.

3. Model Training: XYZ Electronics uses deep learning techniques to train a convolutional neural network (CNN) on the annotated image dataset. The CNN learns to recognize patterns and features associated with different types of defects in TV components.

4. Model Evaluation: XYZ Electronics evaluates the performance of the trained CNN on a separate validation dataset to ensure that it can accurately detect defects with high precision and recall.

5. Deployment: Once the CNN model achieves satisfactory performance, XYZ Electronics deploys it into its manufacturing process. The model is integrated into the production line to automatically analyze images of TV components and flag any defects for further inspection or rework.

Python Code:
Below is a simplified example of how XYZ Electronics can implement AI-driven quality control using Python and TensorFlow, a popular deep learning framework:

```python
import tensorflow as tf
from tensorflow.keras.models import Sequential
from tensorflow.keras.layers import Conv2D, MaxPooling2D, Flatten, Dense

# Define CNN model architecture
model = Sequential([
```

```
    Conv2D(32, (3, 3), activation='relu', input_shape=(128, 128, 3)),
    MaxPooling2D((2, 2)),
    Conv2D(64, (3, 3), activation='relu'),
    MaxPooling2D((2, 2)),
    Conv2D(128, (3, 3), activation='relu'),
    MaxPooling2D((2, 2)),
    Flatten(),
    Dense(128, activation='relu'),
    Dense(1, activation='sigmoid')
])

# Compile model
model.compile(optimizer='adam',
        loss='binary_crossentropy',
        metrics=['accuracy'])

# Train model (code for training the model would go here)

# Save model
model.save('defect_detection_model.h5')
```

Results:
By implementing AI-driven quality control, XYZ Electronics achieves significant improvements in the accuracy and efficiency of its manufacturing operations. The computer vision-based system can accurately detect defects in TV components with high precision, reducing the need for manual inspection and ensuring consistent product quality.

Conclusion:
Through the integration of AI technologies into its quality control process, XYZ Electronics enhances its manufacturing capabilities and maintains its competitive edge in the TV industry. The AI-driven system not only improves defect detection accuracy but also increases production efficiency and reduces manufacturing costs, ultimately leading to higher

customer satisfaction and brand reputation.

CASE STUDY: AI-DRIVEN PREDICTIVE MAINTENANCE IN TV MANUFACTURING

Introduction:
ABC Electronics, a leading manufacturer of televisions, is seeking to optimize its manufacturing processes to reduce downtime, increase efficiency, and improve overall productivity. To achieve these goals, ABC Electronics plans to implement AI-driven predictive maintenance in its TV manufacturing facilities.

Objective:
The objective of this project is to leverage artificial intelligence (AI) technologies to predict equipment failures before they occur, allowing ABC Electronics to perform maintenance proactively and prevent costly unplanned downtime. By implementing predictive maintenance, ABC Electronics aims to improve equipment reliability, extend asset lifespan, and optimize maintenance schedules.

Approach:
ABC Electronics adopts the following approach to implement AI-driven predictive maintenance:

1. Data Collection: ABC Electronics collects historical data

from sensors installed on manufacturing equipment, including temperature, vibration, and operating parameters. This data provides insights into the normal operating conditions and failure patterns of the equipment.

2. Data Preprocessing: The collected sensor data is preprocessed to clean and prepare it for analysis. This may involve removing outliers, imputing missing values, and scaling the data to ensure compatibility with the machine learning algorithms.

3. Model Development: ABC Electronics develops machine learning models, such as random forests or recurrent neural networks (RNNs), to analyze the sensor data and predict equipment failures. These models learn patterns and trends in the data to identify early indicators of potential failures.

4. Model Training: The machine learning models are trained using the preprocessed historical data. During training, the models learn to recognize patterns associated with equipment failures and optimize their predictive capabilities.

5. Model Deployment: Once trained, the predictive maintenance models are deployed into production environments. They continuously monitor real-time sensor data from manufacturing equipment and generate alerts when they detect anomalies or deviations from normal operating conditions.

Python Code (Sample for Model Training):
Below is a simplified example of how ABC Electronics can train a random forest classifier for predictive maintenance using Python and scikit-learn:

```python
import pandas as pd
from sklearn.ensemble import RandomForestClassifier
from sklearn.model_selection import train_test_split
from sklearn.metrics import accuracy_score

# Load historical sensor data
```

```
sensor_data = pd.read_csv('sensor_data.csv')

# Preprocess data (e.g., handle missing values, scale features)

# Split data into features and target variable
X = sensor_data.drop(columns=['failure'])
y = sensor_data['failure']

# Split data into training and testing sets
X_train, X_test, y_train, y_test = train_test_split(X, y,
test_size=0.2, random_state=42)

# Train random forest classifier
clf           =           RandomForestClassifier(n_estimators=100,
random_state=42)
clf.fit(X_train, y_train)

# Evaluate model performance
y_pred = clf.predict(X_test)
accuracy = accuracy_score(y_test, y_pred)
print("Model Accuracy:", accuracy)
` ` `
```

Results:
By implementing AI-driven predictive maintenance, ABC Electronics achieves significant improvements in equipment reliability and operational efficiency. The predictive models accurately identify potential equipment failures in advance, allowing maintenance teams to take proactive measures to prevent downtime and maintain optimal production levels.

Conclusion:
Through the implementation of AI-driven predictive maintenance, ABC Electronics transforms its manufacturing operations, reducing costs, and improving overall productivity. By leveraging machine learning algorithms to predict equipment failures before they occur, ABC Electronics demonstrates its commitment to innovation and efficiency in the competitive TV manufacturing industry.

CASE STUDY: AI FOR QUALITY CONTROL IN TV MANUFACTURING

Introduction:
ABC Electronics, a prominent TV manufacturer, aims to enhance its quality control processes using artificial intelligence (AI). The company recognizes the importance of ensuring high product quality and seeks to leverage AI technologies to automate defect detection and improve manufacturing efficiency.

Objective:
The objective of this project is to implement a computer vision-based quality control system that can automatically detect defects in TV components during the manufacturing process. By integrating AI into its quality control process, ABC Electronics aims to reduce human error, increase throughput, and ensure consistent product quality.

Approach:
ABC Electronics adopts the following approach to implement AI for quality control in TV manufacturing:

1. Data Collection: ABC Electronics collects a large dataset of images of TV components, including circuit boards, display panels, and casings, both with and without defects. These images serve as the training data for the AI model.

2. Data Annotation: ABC Electronics annotates the images to

label defects such as scratches, dents, and soldering errors. This step is crucial for training the AI model to accurately identify and classify defects in the images.

3. Model Training: ABC Electronics uses deep learning techniques to train a convolutional neural network (CNN) on the annotated image dataset. The CNN learns to recognize patterns and features associated with different types of defects in TV components.

4. Model Evaluation: ABC Electronics evaluates the performance of the trained CNN on a separate validation dataset to ensure that it can accurately detect defects with high precision and recall.

5. Deployment: Once the CNN model achieves satisfactory performance, ABC Electronics deploys it into its manufacturing process. The model is integrated into the production line to automatically analyze images of TV components and flag any defects for further inspection or rework.

Python Code:
Below is a simplified example of how ABC Electronics can implement AI for quality control using Python and TensorFlow, a popular deep learning framework:

```python
import tensorflow as tf
from tensorflow.keras.models import Sequential
from tensorflow.keras.layers import Conv2D, MaxPooling2D, Flatten, Dense

# Define CNN model architecture
model = Sequential([
    Conv2D(32, (3, 3), activation='relu', input_shape=(128, 128, 3)),
    MaxPooling2D((2, 2)),
    Conv2D(64, (3, 3), activation='relu'),
```

```
    MaxPooling2D((2, 2)),
    Conv2D(128, (3, 3), activation='relu'),
    MaxPooling2D((2, 2)),
    Flatten(),
    Dense(128, activation='relu'),
    Dense(1, activation='sigmoid')
])

# Compile model
model.compile(optimizer='adam',
        loss='binary_crossentropy',
        metrics=['accuracy'])

# Train model (code for training the model would go here)

# Save model
model.save('defect_detection_model.h5')
` ` `
```

Results:
By implementing AI for quality control, ABC Electronics achieves significant improvements in the accuracy and efficiency of its manufacturing operations. The computer vision-based system can accurately detect defects in TV components with high precision, reducing the need for manual inspection and ensuring consistent product quality.

Conclusion:
Through the integration of AI technologies into its quality control process, ABC Electronics enhances its manufacturing capabilities and maintains its competitive edge in the TV industry. The AI-driven system not only improves defect detection accuracy but also increases production efficiency and reduces manufacturing costs, ultimately leading to higher customer satisfaction and brand reputation.

CASE STUDY: IMPLEMENTING AI FOR PERSONALIZED CONTENT RECOMMENDATIONS IN SMART TVS

Introduction:
In the rapidly evolving landscape of television technology, Smart TVs have become a ubiquitous feature in modern households. To stay competitive, TV manufacturers are constantly seeking innovative ways to enhance user experience. One such approach is leveraging artificial intelligence (AI) to deliver personalized content recommendations tailored to individual viewers' preferences.

Objective:
The objective of this project is to implement AI algorithms in Smart TVs to analyze viewing habits, preferences, and other relevant data to provide personalized content recommendations. By understanding users' interests and behaviors, TV manufacturers aim to improve user engagement, satisfaction, and loyalty.

Approach:
The approach involves implementing AI-driven recommendation systems within Smart TVs. The process can be broken down into the following steps:

1. Data Collection: Smart TVs collect data on users' viewing history, preferences, interactions with the TV interface, and other relevant information. This data may include which channels or streaming services users frequently access, genres they prefer, time of day they watch TV, and so on.

2. Data Processing: The collected data is processed and analyzed to extract meaningful insights about users' preferences and behavior. This may involve data cleaning, feature engineering, and other preprocessing steps to prepare the data for use in recommendation algorithms.

3. AI Recommendation Algorithms: Various AI algorithms, such as collaborative filtering, content-based filtering, and hybrid approaches, are employed to generate personalized content recommendations. These algorithms analyze the processed data to predict which TV shows, movies, or other content users are likely to enjoy based on their historical preferences and behavior.

4. User Interface Integration: The personalized recommendations generated by the AI algorithms are integrated into the Smart TV user interface. This may involve creating a dedicated recommendations section on the home screen, displaying personalized content suggestions alongside traditional TV listings, or even providing recommendations via voice commands.

5. Feedback Loop: The recommendation system continuously learns and improves over time through a feedback loop. Users' interactions with the recommended content, such as whether they watch, like, or dislike suggested shows, are tracked

and used to update the AI algorithms and refine future recommendations.

Python Code (Sample for Collaborative Filtering):
Below is a simplified example of how collaborative filtering, one of the popular recommendation algorithms, can be implemented in Python using the Surprise library:

```python
from surprise import Dataset, Reader
from surprise.model_selection import train_test_split
from surprise import SVD
from surprise import accuracy

# Load dataset (replace 'path_to_dataset' with the actual file path)
reader = Reader(line_format='user item rating', sep=',')
data = Dataset.load_from_file('path_to_dataset', reader=reader)

# Split dataset into training and testing sets
trainset, testset = train_test_split(data, test_size=0.2, random_state=42)

# Train the SVD algorithm
algo = SVD()
algo.fit(trainset)

# Make predictions on the test set
predictions = algo.test(testset)

# Calculate RMSE (Root Mean Squared Error)
accuracy.rmse(predictions)
```

Results:
By implementing AI for personalized content recommendations, TV manufacturers can enhance user engagement and satisfaction. Users benefit from discovering new content tailored to their interests, while TV manufacturers

benefit from increased viewer retention and loyalty.

Conclusion:

AI-driven personalized content recommendations represent a significant opportunity for Smart TV manufacturers to differentiate their products and provide added value to users. By leveraging AI algorithms to analyze user data and generate personalized recommendations, Smart TVs can deliver a more engaging and tailored viewing experience, ultimately driving customer satisfaction and brand loyalty.

CASE STUDY: IMPLEMENTING AI FOR SMART TV VOICE CONTROL

Introduction:
In the era of smart technology, TVs have evolved beyond traditional viewing devices to become intelligent hubs for entertainment and information. One of the latest advancements in TV technology is the integration of artificial intelligence (AI) for voice control. This case study explores how AI can be implemented in TVs to enable voice control functionalities, enhancing user experience and convenience.

Objective:
The objective of this project is to implement AI-driven voice control features in smart TVs, allowing users to interact with their TVs using natural language commands. By leveraging AI, TV manufacturers aim to provide a seamless and intuitive user interface, enabling users to control various TV functions, access content, and even perform internet searches using voice commands.

Approach:
The approach involves implementing AI-powered natural language processing (NLP) algorithms within smart TVs to interpret and respond to user voice commands. The process can

be outlined as follows:

1. Speech Recognition: The TV's microphone captures the user's voice commands, which are then processed by a speech recognition system. This system converts the spoken words into text, enabling the TV to understand the user's commands.

2. Natural Language Understanding (NLU): The text-based voice commands are passed through an NLP algorithm, which analyzes the syntax and semantics of the user's input to extract the user's intent. This step involves parsing the text and identifying the relevant keywords and phrases.

3. Command Execution: Based on the interpreted user intent, the TV executes the corresponding action. This could involve changing channels, adjusting volume, launching apps, searching for content, or performing other tasks requested by the user.

4. Feedback and Response: The TV provides feedback to the user to confirm that the command has been understood and executed successfully. This may include visual feedback on the screen, such as displaying a confirmation message or executing the requested action.

5. Continuous Learning: The AI system continuously learns and improves over time based on user interactions and feedback. This allows the TV to adapt to individual users' preferences and speech patterns, improving the accuracy and responsiveness of the voice control system over time.

Python Code (Sample for Speech Recognition using SpeechRecognition library):
Below is a simplified example of how speech recognition can be implemented in Python using the SpeechRecognition library:

```python
import speech_recognition as sr
```

```
# Create a recognizer object
recognizer = sr.Recognizer()

# Capture audio from microphone
with sr.Microphone() as source:
    print("Listening...")
    audio = recognizer.listen(source)

# Convert speech to text
try:
    text = recognizer.recognize_google(audio)
    print("You said:", text)
except sr.UnknownValueError:
    print("Sorry, could not understand audio.")
except sr.RequestError as e:
    print("Could not request results; {0}".format(e))
` ` `
```

Results:
By implementing AI for smart TV voice control, TV manufacturers can offer users a more intuitive and convenient way to interact with their TVs. Users benefit from hands-free control, allowing them to navigate menus, search for content, and control TV functions using simple voice commands.

Conclusion:
AI-powered voice control represents a significant advancement in smart TV technology, providing users with a more natural and seamless interaction experience. By integrating AI algorithms for speech recognition and natural language understanding, smart TVs can offer enhanced functionality and convenience, driving user satisfaction and loyalty.

CASE STUDY: ENHANCING TV VIEWING EXPERIENCE WITH AI-DRIVEN CONTENT RECOMMENDATIONS

Introduction:
In the era of digital streaming and on-demand content, viewers are faced with an overwhelming array of options when it comes to selecting what to watch on TV. To address this challenge and enhance the TV viewing experience, TV manufacturers are leveraging artificial intelligence (AI) to deliver personalized content recommendations tailored to individual preferences. This case study explores how AI can be implemented in TVs to provide personalized content recommendations, ultimately improving user engagement and satisfaction.

Objective:
The objective of this project is to implement AI algorithms in TVs to analyze viewing habits, preferences, and other relevant data to provide personalized content recommendations. By understanding users' interests and behaviors, TV manufacturers aim to improve user engagement, satisfaction, and loyalty.

Approach:

The approach involves implementing AI-driven recommendation systems within Smart TVs. The process can be broken down into the following steps:

1. Data Collection: Smart TVs collect data on users' viewing history, preferences, interactions with the TV interface, and other relevant information. This data may include which channels or streaming services users frequently access, genres they prefer, time of day they watch TV, and so on.

2. Data Processing: The collected data is processed and analyzed to extract meaningful insights about users' preferences and behavior. This may involve data cleaning, feature engineering, and other preprocessing steps to prepare the data for use in recommendation algorithms.

3. AI Recommendation Algorithms: Various AI algorithms, such as collaborative filtering, content-based filtering, and hybrid approaches, are employed to generate personalized content recommendations. These algorithms analyze the processed data to predict which TV shows, movies, or other content users are likely to enjoy based on their historical preferences and behavior.

4. User Interface Integration: The personalized recommendations generated by the AI algorithms are integrated into the Smart TV user interface. This may involve creating a dedicated recommendations section on the home screen, displaying personalized content suggestions alongside traditional TV listings, or even providing recommendations via voice commands.

5. Feedback Loop: The recommendation system continuously learns and improves over time through a feedback loop. Users' interactions with the recommended content, such as whether they watch, like, or dislike suggested shows, are tracked

and used to update the AI algorithms and refine future recommendations.

Python Code (Sample for Collaborative Filtering):
Below is a simplified example of how collaborative filtering, one of the popular recommendation algorithms, can be implemented in Python using the Surprise library:

```python
from surprise import Dataset, Reader
from surprise.model_selection import train_test_split
from surprise import SVD
from surprise import accuracy

# Load dataset (replace 'path_to_dataset' with the actual file path)
reader = Reader(line_format='user item rating', sep=',')
data = Dataset.load_from_file('path_to_dataset', reader=reader)

# Split dataset into training and testing sets
trainset, testset = train_test_split(data, test_size=0.2, random_state=42)

# Train the SVD algorithm
algo = SVD()
algo.fit(trainset)

# Make predictions on the test set
predictions = algo.test(testset)

# Calculate RMSE (Root Mean Squared Error)
accuracy.rmse(predictions)
```

Results:
By implementing AI for personalized content recommendations, TV manufacturers can enhance user engagement and satisfaction. Users benefit from discovering new content tailored to their interests, while TV manufacturers

benefit from increased viewer retention and loyalty.

Conclusion:

AI-driven personalized content recommendations represent a significant opportunity for Smart TV manufacturers to differentiate their products and provide added value to users. By leveraging AI algorithms to analyze user data and generate personalized recommendations, Smart TVs can deliver a more engaging and tailored viewing experience, ultimately driving customer satisfaction and brand loyalty.

CASE STUDY: IMPLEMENTING AI FOR VOICE RECOGNITION IN SMART TVS

Introduction:

In the rapidly advancing landscape of technology, Smart TVs have become more than just devices for viewing television programs. They have transformed into smart hubs for entertainment, communication, and home automation. One of the latest advancements in Smart TV technology is the integration of artificial intelligence (AI) for voice recognition. This case study explores how AI can be implemented in Smart TVs to enable voice control functionalities, enhancing user experience and convenience.

Objective:

The objective of this project is to implement AI-driven voice recognition features in Smart TVs, allowing users to interact with their TVs using natural language commands. By leveraging AI, TV manufacturers aim to provide a seamless and intuitive user interface, enabling users to control various TV functions, access content, and perform internet searches using voice commands.

Approach:
The approach involves implementing AI-powered natural language processing (NLP) algorithms within Smart TVs to interpret and respond to user voice commands. The process can be outlined as follows:

1. Speech Recognition: The TV's microphone captures the user's voice commands, which are then processed by a speech recognition system. This system converts the spoken words into text, enabling the TV to understand the user's commands.

2. Natural Language Understanding (NLU): The text-based voice commands are passed through an NLP algorithm, which analyzes the syntax and semantics of the user's input to extract the user's intent. This step involves parsing the text and identifying the relevant keywords and phrases.

3. Command Execution: Based on the interpreted user intent, the TV executes the corresponding action. This could involve changing channels, adjusting volume, launching apps, searching for content, or performing other tasks requested by the user.

4. Feedback and Response: The TV provides feedback to the user to confirm that the command has been understood and executed successfully. This may include visual feedback on the screen, such as displaying a confirmation message or executing the requested action.

5. Continuous Learning: The AI system continuously learns and improves over time based on user interactions and feedback. This allows the TV to adapt to individual users' preferences and speech patterns, improving the accuracy and responsiveness of the voice control system over time.

Python Code (Sample for Speech Recognition using SpeechRecognition library):
Below is a simplified example of how speech recognition can be

implemented in Python using the SpeechRecognition library:

```python
import speech_recognition as sr

# Create a recognizer object
recognizer = sr.Recognizer()

# Capture audio from microphone
with sr.Microphone() as source:
    print("Listening...")
    audio = recognizer.listen(source)

# Convert speech to text
try:
    text = recognizer.recognize_google(audio)
    print("You said:", text)
except sr.UnknownValueError:
    print("Sorry, could not understand audio.")
except sr.RequestError as e:
    print("Could not request results; {0}".format(e))
```

Results:
By implementing AI for smart TV voice recognition, TV manufacturers can offer users a more intuitive and convenient way to interact with their TVs. Users benefit from hands-free control, allowing them to navigate menus, search for content, and control TV functions using simple voice commands.

Conclusion:
AI-powered voice recognition represents a significant advancement in Smart TV technology, providing users with a more natural and seamless interaction experience. By integrating AI algorithms for speech recognition and natural language understanding, Smart TVs can offer enhanced functionality and convenience, driving user satisfaction and loyalty.

CASE STUDY: IMPLEMENTING AI FOR CONTENT RECOMMENDATIONS IN SMART TVS

Introduction:
In today's digital age, Smart TVs have become more than just a means of watching television shows. With the abundance of streaming services and content options available, users often face the challenge of finding relevant and engaging content to watch. To address this challenge, TV manufacturers are leveraging artificial intelligence (AI) to provide personalized content recommendations tailored to individual preferences. This case study explores how AI can be implemented in Smart TVs to enhance the content discovery experience for users.

Objective:
The objective of this project is to implement AI algorithms in Smart TVs to analyze user preferences, viewing habits, and historical data to provide personalized content recommendations. By leveraging AI, TV manufacturers aim to improve user engagement, satisfaction, and retention by delivering content that aligns with users' interests.

Approach:

The approach involves implementing AI-driven recommendation systems within Smart TVs. The process can be outlined as follows:

1. Data Collection: Smart TVs collect data on users' viewing history, preferences, ratings, and interactions with the TV interface. This data may include information such as which shows or movies users watch, genres they prefer, time of day they watch TV, and feedback they provide on content.

2. Data Processing: The collected data is processed and analyzed to extract meaningful insights about users' preferences and behavior. This may involve data cleaning, feature engineering, and other preprocessing steps to prepare the data for use in recommendation algorithms.

3. AI Recommendation Algorithms: Various AI algorithms, such as collaborative filtering, content-based filtering, and hybrid approaches, are employed to generate personalized content recommendations. These algorithms analyze the processed data to predict which TV shows, movies, or other content users are likely to enjoy based on their historical preferences and behavior.

4. User Interface Integration: The personalized recommendations generated by the AI algorithms are integrated into the Smart TV user interface. This may involve creating a dedicated recommendations section on the home screen, displaying personalized content suggestions alongside traditional TV listings, or even providing recommendations via voice commands.

5. Feedback Loop: The recommendation system continuously learns and improves over time through a feedback loop. Users' interactions with the recommended content, such as whether they watch, like, or dislike suggested shows, are tracked and used to update the AI algorithms and refine future recommendations.

Python Code (Sample for Collaborative Filtering):
Below is a simplified example of how collaborative filtering, one of the popular recommendation algorithms, can be implemented in Python using the Surprise library:

```python
from surprise import Dataset, Reader
from surprise.model_selection import train_test_split
from surprise import SVD
from surprise import accuracy

# Load dataset (replace 'path_to_dataset' with the actual file path)
reader = Reader(line_format='user item rating', sep=',')
data = Dataset.load_from_file('path_to_dataset', reader=reader)

# Split dataset into training and testing sets
trainset, testset = train_test_split(data, test_size=0.2, random_state=42)

# Train the SVD algorithm
algo = SVD()
algo.fit(trainset)

# Make predictions on the test set
predictions = algo.test(testset)

# Calculate RMSE (Root Mean Squared Error)
accuracy.rmse(predictions)
```

Results:
By implementing AI for personalized content recommendations, TV manufacturers can enhance user engagement and satisfaction. Users benefit from discovering new content tailored to their interests, while TV manufacturers benefit from increased viewer retention and loyalty.

Conclusion:

AI-driven personalized content recommendations represent a significant opportunity for Smart TV manufacturers to differentiate their products and provide added value to users. By leveraging AI algorithms to analyze user data and generate personalized recommendations, Smart TVs can deliver a more engaging and tailored viewing experience, ultimately driving customer satisfaction and brand loyalty.

CASE STUDY: AI-ENABLED VOICE RECOGNITION IN SMART TVS

Introduction:
In today's rapidly evolving technological landscape, Smart TVs have become an integral part of modern living rooms, offering users a plethora of entertainment options. To enhance user experience and accessibility, TV manufacturers are increasingly integrating artificial intelligence (AI) into their devices. One notable application of AI in Smart TVs is voice recognition, allowing users to interact with their TVs using natural language commands. This case study explores the implementation of AI-enabled voice recognition in Smart TVs and its benefits for users.

Objective:
The objective of this project is to implement AI-driven voice recognition features in Smart TVs, enabling users to control various functions, access content, and perform tasks using voice commands. By leveraging AI, TV manufacturers aim to provide a seamless and intuitive user interface, enhancing user convenience and accessibility.

Approach:
The approach involves implementing AI-powered natural language processing (NLP) algorithms within Smart TVs to

interpret and respond to user voice commands. The process can be outlined as follows:

1. Speech Recognition: The TV's microphone captures the user's voice commands, which are then processed by a speech recognition system. This system converts the spoken words into text, enabling the TV to understand the user's commands.

2. Natural Language Understanding (NLU): The text-based voice commands are passed through an NLP algorithm, which analyzes the syntax and semantics of the user's input to extract the user's intent. This step involves parsing the text and identifying the relevant keywords and phrases.

3. Command Execution: Based on the interpreted user intent, the TV executes the corresponding action. This could involve changing channels, adjusting volume, launching apps, searching for content, or performing other tasks requested by the user.

4. Feedback and Response: The TV provides feedback to the user to confirm that the command has been understood and executed successfully. This may include visual feedback on the screen, such as displaying a confirmation message or executing the requested action.

5. Continuous Learning: The AI system continuously learns and improves over time based on user interactions and feedback. This allows the TV to adapt to individual users' preferences and speech patterns, improving the accuracy and responsiveness of the voice control system over time.

Python Code (Sample for Speech Recognition using SpeechRecognition library):
Below is a simplified example of how speech recognition can be implemented in Python using the SpeechRecognition library:

```python
import speech_recognition as sr
```

```
# Create a recognizer object
recognizer = sr.Recognizer()

# Capture audio from microphone
with sr.Microphone() as source:
    print("Listening...")
    audio = recognizer.listen(source)

# Convert speech to text
try:
    text = recognizer.recognize_google(audio)
    print("You said:", text)
except sr.UnknownValueError:
    print("Sorry, could not understand audio.")
except sr.RequestError as e:
    print("Could not request results; {0}".format(e))
` ` `
```

Results:
By implementing AI for voice recognition, Smart TV manufacturers can offer users a more intuitive and convenient way to interact with their TVs. Users benefit from hands-free control, allowing them to navigate menus, search for content, and control TV functions using simple voice commands.

Conclusion:
AI-powered voice recognition represents a significant advancement in Smart TV technology, providing users with a more natural and seamless interaction experience. By integrating AI algorithms for speech recognition and natural language understanding, Smart TVs can offer enhanced functionality and convenience, driving user satisfaction and loyalty.

CASE STUDY: IMPLEMENTING AI FOR ENERGY-EFFICIENT TV MANUFACTURING

Introduction:
As concerns about global warming and environmental sustainability continue to rise, industries are increasingly seeking ways to reduce their carbon footprint and energy consumption. The TV manufacturing industry is no exception. This case study explores the implementation of AI in TV manufacturing processes to enhance energy efficiency and reduce environmental impact.

Objective:
The objective of this project is to leverage AI technologies to optimize TV manufacturing processes, leading to energy savings and reduced greenhouse gas emissions. By implementing AI-driven solutions, TV manufacturers aim to minimize energy consumption during production while maintaining high-quality standards.

Approach:
The approach involves integrating AI into various aspects of TV manufacturing processes to improve efficiency and

reduce energy usage. This includes optimizing manufacturing equipment, improving supply chain management, and enhancing product design to minimize energy requirements.

1. AI-driven Equipment Optimization: AI algorithms are used to analyze data from manufacturing equipment sensors to optimize energy usage and production efficiency. Machine learning models can predict equipment failures, allowing for proactive maintenance to prevent energy-wasting downtime.

2. Supply Chain Optimization: AI is employed to optimize the supply chain, reducing transportation-related emissions and energy consumption. Predictive analytics help optimize inventory levels and distribution routes, minimizing energy-intensive transportation activities.

3. Product Design Optimization: AI-powered design optimization tools are used to create energy-efficient TV models. By analyzing various design parameters, AI algorithms can identify opportunities to reduce energy consumption during both manufacturing and usage phases.

4. Smart Energy Management: AI-enabled energy management systems are implemented in manufacturing facilities to monitor and control energy usage in real-time. These systems optimize energy distribution and usage based on production demands and external factors such as weather conditions and energy prices.

Python Code (Sample for Predictive Maintenance using AI):
Below is a simplified example of how predictive maintenance using AI can be implemented in Python using machine learning libraries:

```python
import pandas as pd
from sklearn.ensemble import RandomForestClassifier
from sklearn.model_selection import train_test_split
```

```
from sklearn.metrics import accuracy_score

# Load historical sensor data
sensor_data = pd.read_csv('sensor_data.csv')

# Preprocess data (e.g., handle missing values, scale features)

# Split data into features and target variable
X = sensor_data.drop(columns=['failure'])
y = sensor_data['failure']

# Split data into training and testing sets
X_train, X_test, y_train, y_test = train_test_split(X, y,
test_size=0.2, random_state=42)

# Train random forest classifier
clf = RandomForestClassifier(n_estimators=100,
random_state=42)
clf.fit(X_train, y_train)

# Evaluate model performance
y_pred = clf.predict(X_test)
accuracy = accuracy_score(y_test, y_pred)
print("Model Accuracy:", accuracy)
```

Results:
By implementing AI-driven solutions in TV manufacturing processes, manufacturers can achieve significant energy savings and reduce their environmental impact. This not only contributes to mitigating global warming but also enhances cost-effectiveness and sustainability in the industry.

Conclusion:
The integration of AI technologies in TV manufacturing holds great promise for improving energy efficiency and sustainability, thereby indirectly contributing to the fight against global warming. By optimizing manufacturing processes, supply chains, and product designs, AI-driven

solutions help reduce energy consumption and greenhouse gas emissions, aligning with broader environmental goals.

www.ingramcontent.com/pod-product-compliance
Lightning Source LLC
LaVergne TN
LVHW052059060326
832903LV00061B/3623